Cracking the Modern PM Interview

Landing a Product Manager Job in Today's Tech Market

Alex Trottier

Contents:

1. Introduction: The Uncertain Path of the Modern Product Manager

Goals of this book

Landing a product management job at a good company appears to be tougher than ever. The market as well as the role itself have gone through transformations in recent quarters and years, this makes understanding what employers want harder than ever. As industry sentiment suggests that successful product managers are critical to company success, it's no wonder so many are attracted to the official title and the allure of innovation. But being a product manager, especially in the software space, is incredibly uncertain.

How do you handle such a transformative phase? How do you as an experienced or new Product Manager tackle these changes? How do you make sure you put as many chances on your side to land that dream role?

This book is your blueprint for successfully preparing you for any product management interview.

Product managers do many things, but they are often relied on to bridge business, user, and technical domains to craft and communicate a product from its nascent beginnings within the moldy basement of a startup to its mature form in a billion-dollar behemoth. The know-how and skills required to contribute in such a capacity at a high level have never been better understood. They are so well understood, in fact, and are no longer reserved for an elite squad of intellectuals in the employ of governments and their corporations. We hope this guide touches on some viable strategies for potential product managers and invites them to begin thinking differently in ways that are made possible by the content of this book.

This book is designed to prepare you for **real-world challenges** and demonstrate what employers are looking for in their product management teams. ☐ ☐

This book is about anticipating answers. If you come prepared to the interview, knowing what's important for the interviewer, you then have a huge advantage over your competition. In this book we aim to give you the right context of today's product development teams. This helps you understand what is important and can tailor your interview answers according to the right context presented before you.

You cannot make up experience. You can, however, find the tools to best present yourself during the interviews. If you already understand the context of the company, the product, the interviewer, this helps you tremendously.

More about the author

Having spent more than two decades building and leading B2B and B2C businesses, I have watched how the product management industry has evolved, and how it demands a nimble jobseeker. I've built product teams and scaled startups and large companies alike. My passion for helping would-be PMs understand the nuances of today's hiring market and the technologies that are driving change – AI being one of the most important – comes from having lived and breathed these shifts. As someone who has hired and mentored hundreds of PMs, I know how difficult it can be for anyone new to the field to navigate the changing winds of tech trends, especially when there are already so many unanswered questions about what is, or is not, expected of a PM. This book is based on data from my conversations with more than 50 of today's top professionals, and my interviews with hundreds of product companies to analyse their job postings. I've never written a book before, and I intend for Cracking the PM Interview to be as practical, real-world advice as you can find – not just to help you hack the PM interview, but to set you up for success in an industry that will continue to change. This is a book that, will give you the tools to thrive in today's product management.

1.1. Why product management is more critical—and more challenging—than ever

More products are being built now than ever before, using cutting-edge technologies like machine learning, AI, and robotics. But as more is asked of product teams, PMs are increasingly responsible for delivering financially successful products. Most product teams deliver products their engineering team can build, but great PMs deliver on market needs, feel the pressure to innovate, and work to innovate faster than the competition. The average SaaS company uses about 120 cloud-based tools, and many of those PMs can directly impact the revenue of products. That's why product management is becoming a part of every team, and not just for those with a 'Product Manager' title.

The nature of the products we are asked to build is driving the skills we need to be great PMs. Because customer expectations are driven by the products they use in their everyday work, our products must fulfill the 'Consumerization of the Enterprise' trend (i.e., be simple, beautiful, easy to use, etc.). This means we have to understand product design principles just as well as our engineering colleagues. Because we've moved from Waterfall to Agile processes, our PMs have to understand a wide breadth of technical jargon. As parts of the world become even more accessible, the importance of understanding markets outside your everyday routine has never been more crucial. Since software can now be copied faster than ever before, our products have to be strategically defensible. With design thinking moving to the forefront of fast growth companies, you'll need to understand brand, UX, and customer journey to differentiate your products from an exponentially crowded marketplace. And as fast growth companies become fast growth public companies, you're expected to understand the mechanics of how a SaaS company works from sales and marketing to revenue recognition and professional services. We now routinely employ people on our teams with hybrid titles like PM/SME and PM/MBA because the role requires a breadth of experience.

Since the early 2000s, the pressure to evolve the PM skills that account for all this has only gotten more difficult. Fifty years is an eternity in marketing. It took weeks into months for the world to introduce fresh takes about the recent observability buzzword. It's quickly innovate or die today. Don't chase fads, but you need to embrace a forward-thinking mentality. Inner change is rapid. Forty-eight percent of us change jobs every 2-3 years. Product management is the 14th fastest growing title, year over year. The skills required to excel in this profession have been quickly evolving, as well. In five years, 97% of our jobs will change due to advances in technology and shifts in how we relate to our colleagues. And this is typical of all titles, not just PMs. You must practice continuous learning if you wish to endure in today's hyper fast-paced workforce. However, whether you've been doing product management for 20 years or just embarking on your first job, the reality of what it is to be a PM—the hard skills, the soft skills, the day-to-day realities—doesn't alter.

1.2. What companies are looking for in modern PM interviews

In modern PM interviews, organizations are looking to assess if a candidate has the skills to be a successful PM. This includes technical product management skills, which can involve work they will do at a strategic, execution, or tactical level. This also includes a candidate's soft skills. Organizations are testing to see if a candidate has analytical reasoning, can provide strong leadership, and can think and plan for customers with a customer-centric mindset. These types of PMs are also well-versed in data and can draw reasonable conclusions from available information to hone strategies and develop products based on company objectives, customer requirements, and efficiency. Hiring PMs also look for a cultural fit. The candidate should have similar motivations and complementary values and goals to the rest of the organization. By and large, organizations perform cross-functional interviews, meaning that the candidate will usually interview with managers in other departments, including sales and human resources, to see if this employee can work across groups and is potentially another good fit for the leaders of those departments.

PM interviews can give an indication of how the company operates and what these executives think of the marketplace and the organization, and how a PM would be expected to perform at the headquarters. Interview formats also include the case study format to flag PMs who have the ability to work across fields and have transferable abilities. These case studies include small doubts, understanding an issue statement, and can deal with alternative outcomes, although these are not always problems with a definitive answer. The interview may also incorporate behavioral questions, such as "Why did you handle this situation in this manner?" to test if there are any issues with the administration and leadership, plus how long before a PM can complete a new position for a later business opportunity. This type of interview will also include resistance in the evaluation, as well as check potential follow-up queries.

1.3. The evolving landscape: From feature management to strategic leadership, including the impact of AI

As the PM role has evolved with the acceleration of market demands, what is expected from the PM role has skyrocketed. No longer are PMs merely box-checking, list-making feature managers; they are expected to understand what and why, developing a business-driven vision and strategy, figuring out product/market fit, charting a path forward, and continually innovating. This evolution is partially due to an age of information and an arsenal of technological tools and techniques, and we will explore and share deep insights into the trajectory of this illuminated path ahead. Artificial intelligence is supercharging many of the current PM responsibilities and expected outcomes driving this narrative. The data-derived presentation of a far-away future first predicted where AI will reimagine strategic business roles of leaders, such as PMs soon to become the Chief

Technology Prophet or Visionary. It is a profitable differentiator for organizations to listen to the needs of the market and respond via technology-driven applications.

AI-driven predictive analytics can identify trends long before they are visible in a product, such as in sourcing data that predicted the rise in automated sleep predictions, often used by hospital diagnostic equipment. Any strategy leader can avoid a nearsighted roadmap and be visionary with the challenging aspect of implementation with the help of distributed ledger technology. The core skill of a PM – vision – is available for free to any interested employee via an auto-updated, live, actual feed to the strategic pulse of the market. Competitive advantage is now where really good vision is calculated to make a positive impact on product managers. Vision development is often locked in stalemate for hours debating feature development or fleshing out breakthroughs with various ideation methods. All of these can be automated, and automation and innovation raise the question: why might that be? It will be the PM transformed into a strategic role leader using distributed ledger technology – a bleeding-edge strategic chain. String enough of these insights together, and the roadmap becomes an initiative to drum up investment effectively rather than the fatal punchline of overheard critiques.

Chapter 2: The Evolving Profile of a Product Manager: Skills and Strategies for Success

2.1 The Changing Landscape of Product Management

In the last two decades, software and technology development have been characterized by rapid innovation and change. From waterfall to Agile to DevOps to cloud, continuous waves of reinvention wash over the world of software development. As a result, the role of product managers (PMs) and their influence within product and technology development has also changed substantially. Skills and strategies needed to be a successful product manager five years ago are constantly evolving.

Other factors such as demand, organizational dynamics, global marketplaces, and developing crises create shifts in product and technology development. Many professions borrow models and techniques from product management, making it a versatile field. This section explores modern product management thinking and highlights how professionals need to respond to industry changes.

2.2 The Influence of Technology on the Role of Product Managers

Historically, product managers served as the liaison between users and cross-functional engineering teams. Now, they often act as in-house business owners, crafting strategies for business and marketing. The introduction of AI, machine learning, and data analytics has reshaped product development, particularly around personalization and customer insights. This shift means modern product managers need a strong grasp of technology to enhance product and business strategies.

2.3 Key Skills and Attributes of the Modern Product Manager

The skill set of a PM has to constantly evolve. A product manager has to be able to respond to an ever-changing environment. A product manager needs to be agile and flexible to meet changing demands in the market. A product manager needs to have resilience to thrive in the face of challenges. A product manager must also be able to balance data-driven decision making with creative thinking to produce unique products for the market and compete with other products. A product manager needs a mindset of servant leadership to bring people together and build a cohesive team.

Furthermore, today's product manager is not just expected to execute, but also to think strategically and lead with a vision. The PM is often called upon to switch between tactical decisions and high-level strategic thinking. A strong PM should be good at making decisions, taking into account the trade-offs between two or more options and choosing the ones that make most sense in the context of the short-term deliverables and long-term goals. By understanding the business context and how each feature affects revenues, customer satisfaction and brand image, the PM should be able to deliver products that carve a distinct place for themselves in the market, and create a fan-base of loyal users.

Besides, today's PM must be able to navigate the challenges of digital transformation, new technologies and emerging consumer expectations. They must identify opportunities to grow, apply data analytics, and learn about new tools and methods. Whether it's working Agile, deriving insights from data about user behaviour, or leveraging artificial intelligence to enhance product usability, the PM who succeeds is constantly innovating at the leading edge, guiding the team to do the same.

2.4 Adaptability and Agility in a Fast-Paced Tech Environment

The defining trait of the modern tech environment is flexibility. As customer needs change, PMs must be agile in finding new ways to deliver product, and must be able to make rapid decisions and iterative go-to-market plans in a world that is characterised by rapidly shifting technological adoption rates. There are many stories of PMs who veered off course into an offshoot of their original idea and succeeded because of their flexibility.

A great PM can quickly shift course, without losing sight of the shared vision The tech world is filled with new competitors who can crop up overnight, as well as with technological changes that can completely flip markets. A great PM needs to be nimble, moving quickly to adjust product features or the marketing messaging of a product, or even changing the entire product plan. In some cases, it's not just about engineering a response to change. The best PMs can smell change before it happens, such as signs of a market shift, customer feedback or new technological developments. They're able to quickly pivot and reorient their strategies, sometimes before change takes place.

Also, modern product management is inherently iterative. The days of having long, infrequent development cycles have given way to short, frequent release cycles where teams can push out a new feature, learn from user feedback, and quickly iterate. Agile and Lean methodologies are integral in today's world and central to this way of working. Teams are constantly experimenting, learning, and iterating. PMs need to adopt this mindset and facilitate a culture that allows for experimentation, and even failure, and treats it as an opportunity to learn, rather than a set-back.

Pivoting also applies to how PMs lead and manage their teams. In a fast-paced environment, the ability to pivot quickly needs to be paired with a strong ability to communicate and coordinate with our teams. PMs need to make sure that their teams are onboard, understand why pivots happen so quickly and can quickly adapt their work without losing their motivation. We need to set up our teams to be cross-functional teams that collaborate, learn together, share information and solve problems together. By having a culture that fosters this kind of rapid iteration, our pivots will be easier and our teams will be more successful.

Adaptability in a tech environment also entails being open to learning and unlearning. Being ready to learn new tools, frameworks and technologies as they come along, staying abreast of industry trends and being open to new ways of doing things are crucial to a PM's success. The constant state of learning allows them to lead their teams and their stakeholders, make well-informed decisions, and keep their products leading edge.

2.5 Leadership and Team Management in Cross-Functional Settings

A modern PM is an executor of a product strategy – of a company's strategy – who must manage teams of people across the organisation. Navigating cross-functional conflict requires great leadership skills, and motivation is the key to delivering successful market launches. Product management leadership is about conflict resolution and building trustful teams.

 The winning PM is someone who sits between the engineering, design, marketing and sales teams, and works to get the teams to agree with a single product vision. This requires familiarity not only with each functional group's priorities, but also with the unique argot of each – and the skill to translate it into something human-sounding and relatable. A good PM is quick to switch between technical and business language, reducing the risk of mishaps through a good understanding of the details and nuances of both worlds. Finally, this cross-functional alignment is important for keeping the momentum going, especially with respect to product development, which necessitates knowledge and buy-in across disciplines.

Fostering a multifaceted team means managing different perspectives, skill sets and working styles. For a modern PM, conflict resolution is a key skill, making sure that disagreements do not derail discussion, but serve as a means for the team to move forward. To achieve this, a PM needs to create an open and respectful environment, so that team members feel comfortable sharing their ideas and concerns. The PM needs to be a mediator of differences of opinion, and find ways to arrive at a solution that will align with the product goals. Trust is important here; it creates a collaborative atmosphere where each team member feels valued and invested in the success of the product.

In addition, motivation and enthusiasm are key to moving a product idea from the drawing board to market. The best PMs know how to motivate their teams, tying the day-to-day tasks to a higher mission, and making it clear how the team members play a role in creating something important and useful. They leverage different styles of leadership depending on the situation – including a more directive approach when quick decisions are needed, and pulling back when they need their team members to drive a specific task. This combination of direction and delegation not only motivates the team but it also encourages innovation. Innovation is necessary to create competitive products.

Modern leadership in product management also means leading through change and ambiguity: from pivoting a product strategy, being able to adapt to unexpected technical challenges, or adjusting to market feedback. PMs need to be resilient and proactive, prepared to lead their team through periods of ambiguity – and when they can, provide clarity along the way. This means preparing the team for uncertainty by setting realistic expectations, communicating challenges and setbacks transparently, and celebrating wins along the way, big and small.

A PM's leadership is external to the teams they work with, and involves customers, partners and suppliers. This aspect of leading involves building relationships so that these groups can provide insights, access to resources and ensuring that the product is built to succeed in the market. Good PMs are the voice of the product, articulating what it offers to these groups, but also listening to feedback so that the product can be continually improved.

2.6 Effective Communication and Stakeholder Engagement

Product managers serve as the bridge between various stakeholders, including customers, executives, and development teams. Effective communication is essential to aligning goals and ensuring the product vision is clear. Techniques like product management councils help PMs collaborate across teams and drive innovation. Active listening and stakeholder engagement throughout the product lifecycle reduce risks and foster successful outcomes.

Effective stakeholder management also requires transparent communication and setting clear expectations from the start. Regular updates through newsletters or dashboards keep all parties informed and aligned. PMs often use techniques like stakeholder mapping to identify key influencers and decision-makers, ensuring focused engagement and minimizing roadblocks. Building trust is essential, as is managing conflicting interests diplomatically.

Chapter 3: Strategies for Success in Modern Product Manager Interviews

3.1 Behavioral Questions: What Companies Expect from You

Behavioral questions form the majority of interviews you will receive, even in tech companies. Why? Companies are looking for different skills and attitudes, which they associate with traits responsible for success. A PM should be resilient, able to recover quickly from setbacks, and turn challenges into opportunities. The idea of PM interviews as survival-based is misleading. Unlike competitions, interviews offer multiple chances to prove your abilities across different skill sets. Embrace the opportunity to showcase yourself, reflect honestly, and recall times when you exceeded your limits.

As a PM, you will rely on your communication skills and past successes and failures. While big successes are valuable, well-handled failures can offer important learning points. Understanding the behaviors and qualities companies seek in a PM candidate is essential. Companies often provide information about their ideal PM candidate, so abstract the qualities they are looking for, and ensure that you align with the company's values during interviews.

3.2 Understanding What Companies Expect: Behavioral Questions

Behavioral questions are designed to assess a candidate's potential fit for a team and company culture. Companies ask these questions to gauge core competencies like teamwork, leadership, adaptability, conflict resolution, communication, handling pressure, and vision. These questions help measure personality traits and how candidates approach various situations.

To prepare for a behavioral interview, understand the objective behind each question and review common questions the company has asked in the past. Some companies use structured interview processes, where interviewers are already familiar with certain topics. Thorough preparation is key to handling these types of interviews effectively.

3.3 Handling Technical Questions without a Technical Background

In product manager interviews, it is increasingly common to encounter difficult technical questions, even if the position isn't heavily technical. This can be challenging for candidates without a technical background. However, the key isn't about coding or solving the problem outright, but rather demonstrating analytical thinking and collaboration.

In these situations, it's important to ask clarifying questions and engage the interviewer by showing how you think through problems. Understanding that you have resources—such as colleagues to consult—is vital, as product managers are not traditionally expected to be deeply technical. Tech companies are increasingly embracing product-led approaches, expanding the net for PM candidates.

3.4 Effective Problem Solving: Case Studies and Whiteboarding

Case studies and whiteboarding are common ways to assess a PM's problem-solving, structured thinking, and logical reasoning skills. Case studies typically reflect real-world scenarios that the interviewer has encountered or popular business cases from schools. These exercises test your ability to think through problems and develop practical, measurable solutions.

Whiteboarding simulates a discussion, where the candidate visually presents their reasoning and thought process to the interviewer. This method allows PM candidates to demonstrate their ability to communicate complex ideas and approach problems systematically. Practicing case studies and whiteboarding techniques will give you a competitive edge in PM interviews.è

Whiteboarding exercises also reflect the collaborative aspect of a PM's role, simulating how you might guide team discussions and make decisions under pressure.

3.5 Mastering the STARR Method for Behavioral Interviews

The STARR method (Situation, Task, Action, Results, Reflection) is a structured approach for answering behavioral questions in interviews. The Situation sets the context, the Task outlines the problem or project, the Action explains what you did, the Results show the impact of your actions, and the Reflection highlights what you learned.

By using the STARR method, candidates can structure their answers to ensure clarity and cohesion. This approach helps demonstrate self-awareness, adaptability, and coachability. Practicing the STARR method will improve your ability to deliver consistent, impactful stories in interviews.

Chapter 4: Mastering Product Design Questions in PM Interviews

Product design questions are a staple of product management interviews. But there's more to these questions than just coming up with solutions to user problems; they test your broader product management skills. These questions are meant to test your overall ability to come up with solutions as a product manager, to think on your feet, to use strategic thinking, and to convince the interviewer that you can solve the challenges of the job at hand. Effective PMs aren't just expected to come up with a cool solution, but to do so in a way that explains precisely why it's the right solution, so that other people on the team – especially those focused on business success – can see why and buy in.

This chapter is dedicated to how exactly to approach product design questions, what pitfalls to avoid, which frameworks you should leverage and how, in order to show that you can generate creative ideas, but also bring analytical rigour and skill to sifting through them, differentiating between those that bring real, lasting customer value and those that don't. The methods described here should apply equally well whether your task is to design something from scratch or iterate an existing product.

4.1 Why Product Design Questions Matter

But product design is also the heart of product management, because the art of problem-solving must be grounded in the science of understanding your users. If an interviewer asks you product design questions, you won't necessarily need to conjure up clever new ideas. Instead, you'll be asked to demonstrate how you think – to show how you process information to deliver a user-first solution. The best product managers not only think critically but also demonstrate an intuitive understanding of users.

The task in the interview is not simply to generate ideas, but to show the interviewer how you think, To succeed, your answer has to be inspired, but also organised, evidence-backed, and clear on what customers need. If you have read so far, then this chapter will help you tackle these tricky questions.

4.2 Breaking Down Product Design Questions: A Step-by-Step Approach

At the fundamental level, every question about product design is ultimately about serving a user, so to be good at them, you need to have a structured way to break down the problem and reason through possible solutions in a logical way. Here is a framework that works:

Clarify the Problem: What problem are we solving? And for who? Once those are settled, you can ask yourself: What will it take to solve this problem?

Define Success: Before the brainstorm, take a minute to define success. What are the key results you're hoping to achieve – such as an increased level of user satisfaction, engagement, or revenue?

Start with Possible Solutions – What might the solutions look like? Once you're clear on what the problem is, and what success would look like, come up with some Possible Solutions. What are the big and small things you could do that would make a real difference to the underlying problem? Use the space to go crazy, coming up with as many ideas as possible, and then prune them down to a manageable number.

Balance Trade-offs: Each product decision involves trade-offs – where there are pluses, there are also minuses. Evaluate the trade-off among your solutions – time to market, technical feasibility and risks.

Choose the Best Solution: After considering the various options and their value trade-offs, choose the best solution and explain why it is best. Outline why it addresses user needs and business goals.

4.3 Structuring Your Response: Frameworks for Success

Product design interviews require effective communication with your interviewer, because a well-constructed, clear answer is easier to think and follow than one that feels scattered. There's a set of frameworks that can help you structure your answer:

CIRCLES: Context, Insights, Requirements, Creative solutions, Logical evaluation, Evaluate trade-offs, Summarise This is a well-known framework for helping product managers address design questions, and it can work well for design too: you have a clear discipline to follow that ensures you haven't missed anything.

Jobs-to-Be-Done: Rather than thinking about features, think in terms of the job to be done. This framework keeps you focused on the end goal for the user.

First Principles Thinking: What are the fundamental truths that underlie this problem? Build your solution from the ground up. Great for showing off your creativity and innovation.

4.4 Framing the Problem: Start with Empathy

Before you get to proposed solutions, interviewers want to know whether you can distil a problem into something clear and comprehensible from the user's perspective. Great product design is all about empathy, and your ability to empathise with users will make you stand out. Here's how to do it.

User persona: who has this problem? Figure out who your user is and create a mental picture of them. What do they need? What challenges are they facing? What goals do they have?

Definition of Pain Points: What is the exact problem the user is dealing with and why? Try to think about what is really underneath the symptom.

Put users first: not every user problem is created equal. Work out what kind of pain you need to solve for users first, and why.

4.5 Strategic Thinking: Balancing Stakeholder Needs

Every product decision has ramifications for stakeholders – users, executives, engineering teams and so on. In an interview, you stand a good chance of getting hired if you demonstrate that you can think on a strategic level and balance competing interests, with the user always at the forefront. For example:

Identify all key stakeholders: Who is involved? Users, product teams, salespeople, marketers, upper management? What is their goal, and how will your solution impact them?

Test Business Impact: Does this create business results? Effective design should stem from an understanding and prioritisation of business outcomes, whether that's increasing revenue, reducing customer churn or managing costs.

Present Trade-offs: Product managers live with constraints; tell them about the trade-offs in your design, and why you've prioritised each stakeholder's needs over others.

4.6 Creativity in Product Design: Thinking Outside the Box

The ability to think in creative ways is one of the biggest differentiators in product design interviews. It's not only about solving problems – it's about doing so in ways others haven't. To demonstrate creativity:

Divergent Thinking: Generate a wide range of options by brainstorming freely. The more options begin to crowd your mind, the more likely you'll come up with something truly original.

Reverse Engineering: Look at what is out there already, as products, services, and solve for how you might improve or adapt for your use case.

Question assumptions: Don't be afraid to question prevailing assumptions about how a product currently works (or should work). Asking 'What if?' can be the source of revelatory ideas.

4.7 Communicating Your Ideas: Telling a Compelling Story

The most creative ideas won't get very far if you can't sell them to your interviewers. It's not enough to be creative; you have to present yourself as creative too. Here's how to do it.

Sketch: If you can whiteboard, go for it, but even just sketching out your design can make your ideas clearer and keep your audience engaged.

Use a Story: Tell your idea as a story. What was the issue, how did you go about solving it, and what was the result? Stories stick because they draw a clear line from question to solution.

Expect Pushback: Be prepared for interviewers to challenge your ideas, both before and after your pitch. Plan on responding to questions and pushback, and be ready to defend your solution, but also to pivot based on feedback.

Conclusion:

Product design questions are the perfect opportunity to demonstrate your product thinking, creativity and strategic vision. If you answer these questions with structure, empathy and open mind, you'll be able to prove you have what it takes to envision innovative, user-focused products that solve real problems. This chapter has provided you with the tools to tackle design questions so you can wow in your product management interviews.

Chapter 5: Goal Setting, Execution, OKRs

5.1 Introduction to OKRs

The product management function is integral to all businesses, whether in services, technology, or manufacturing. The product management team is responsible for end-to-end operations, including customer retention in B2B and growth in B2C. Given the broad scope of their responsibilities, it becomes crucial to align the function's objectives with the company's broader goals. OKRs (Objectives and Key Results) serve as a tool to create alignment, focus, and transparency, allowing teams to synchronize their efforts towards common company-wide goals.

5.2 What are OKRs and Why are They Important?

OKR stands for Objective and Key Results. Originally developed at Intel in the 1970s, OKRs have become a popular management tool. The core idea is to align and focus the team around the company's top objectives for the quarter, ensuring that each employee's goals are in sync with the company's strategic vision.

History and Evolution of OKRs

The OKR (Objectives and Key Results) system was developed as a way to increase productivity by synchronising individual work with larger organisational objectives. Inspired by Andy Grove, an early employee at Intel, the OKR was developed in the 1970s, when the firm was quickly becoming the world's foremost personal computer microchip manufacturer, and it emphasised short, medium and long-term goals while testing whether or not these results were being achieved. The OKR allowed Intel to make sense of a rapidly changing technology landscape by establishing what was most important.

OKRs became well-known after John Doerr, formerly of Intel, introduced the concept to Google in the early 2000s. As Google grew, OKRs provided a structured yet flexible framework for achieving focus, accountability and openness throughout the organisation, contributing to its rapid growth. Today, many companies – including LinkedIn, Twitter, Spotify and many others – use OKRs to great effect, adapting the framework as needed to fit their own unique cultures and operating needs.

The OKR methodology has evolved over time as the needs of modern organisations have grown, to include hybrid workforces, agile methodologies, remote teams, and more. OKRs are not just a productivity scorecard but a strategic framework to facilitate alignment, innovation and long-term growth. As organisations have had to become more nimble to adapt to change and uncertainty, the need to pivot and change goals quickly has become critical, making OKRs an agile solution to forward-thinking businesses. Trends to watch would include more frequent check-ins and real-time feedback as well as embedding OKRs into AI-enabled tools that can automate tracking and insights. These should set the scene for the next evolution of OKRs.

5.4 Key Components of OKRs

OKRs comprise two main components:

Objectives: These are clear, inspiring, and challenging goals that guide teams and individuals. Great objectives should stretch the team to achieve meaningful outcomes. What helps here is also focus, allowing the teams to pick one or few objectives to gun for and to channel their entire energy on a few topics.

Key Results: These are measurable outcomes that indicate progress toward an objective. Key results should be specific, trackable, and time-bound to ensure accountability.

In interviews, be ready to show the "flow" of OKRs. Who comes up with the ideas? Who drives and makes final calls when needed? The interviewer wants to know the role you played in setting the strategy and achieving results. They want to know how you used previous frameworks and how you can contribute positively to their own framework. You need to be able to voice clear and concise opinions and experiences when asked.

If you did not work with OKRs, you need to show how decisions were made and how teams were aligned. The interviewer may actually also be interested in how other teams who don't use OKRs work. The point is, it's not so much about the framework you used, but your ability to show how goal setting and alignment was done, what you learned, and what you can now bring to the table.

5.5 Aligning OKRs with Business Goals

OKRs must be aligned with business goals to ensure that every task across the organization is connected back to the company's strategic ambitions. When product managers align OKRs, they create a structure that drives **focus, accountability, and measurable success.** They effectively connect high-level company objectives with the daily activities teams perform, ensuring that resources are spent efficiently and that both the product's current state and its future direction are clear.

The Importance of Alignment in Product Management:

- **Strategic Focus:** Since OKRs are set at the company, division, or business unit level, product managers can ensure that every team is working towards the same strategic goals. This prevents wasted efforts on projects that do not contribute to the broader vision.

- **Clear Accountability:** A clear, explicit link to company-level OKRs allows responsibility to be more easily assigned and tracked. Every team member understands how their work impacts the company's objectives, fostering accountability.

- **Measurable Success:** Effective OKRs link key results to important outcomes, not just tasks. When linked this way, key results become a straightforward, measurable method of tracking progress towards strategic objectives, allowing for claims of impact and adjustments in strategy based on data.

- **Agility and Adaptability:** Aligning OKRs ensures they are flexible in response to external market shifts or changes in company strategy. When company OKRs are clear, product teams can shift and pivot without losing sight of the ultimate target. This adaptability is crucial in fast-moving industries where new competitors and consumer demands can rapidly change the market landscape.

How to Align OKRs with Business Goals:

- **Start with the Company's Strategic Vision:**

  o A good product manager understands the company mission, vision, and long-term goals. Before setting OKRs, they should be well-versed in where the company aims to be over the next five, ten, or fifteen years. This ensures that all objectives and key results are set within the context of the company's long-term trajectory.
  o For instance, if a company's strategic objective is to become a leader in customer experience, a product team might define an objective like **"Improve user satisfaction scores,"** with key results focused on reducing response times, improving onboarding processes, and increasing customer feedback scores.

- **Engage Cross-Functional Teams:**

  o Alignment is not a one-time event but a continuous process. Product managers need to build consensus across cross-functional teams, such as marketing, sales, and engineering, ensuring they all understand the company's priorities and how their efforts contribute to meeting those goals. It's the product manager's role to keep everyone on the same page.

o For example, product managers can run workshops to align team members on OKRs and ensure that each department's objectives complement one another. Such cross-functional planning can expose conflicts or overlaps that might otherwise go unnoticed.

- **Cascading OKRs:**

o Cascading OKRs involve translating company-level OKRs into more specific departmental, team, and individual objectives. This ensures that everyone, from the top down, understands how their work aligns with the company's overall strategy.

o For example, if the company's goal is to **"Increase market share by 15%,"** the product team might set an objective like **"Launch two innovative features targeting emerging market segments,"** with key results such as **"Achieve a 20% adoption rate within six months."**

- **Regular Review and Adjustment:**

o Continuous alignment requires regular check-ins and reviews to assess progress. Product managers might start with quarterly reviews to evaluate if key results are driving the desired outcomes and adjust OKRs as needed. This ongoing review process ensures that goals remain aligned and relevant.

o Because OKRs are frequently reviewed, teams can quickly adapt to new objectives without losing momentum.

- **Using Data to Drive Alignment:**

o Product managers should use data to track progress and validate alignment. Analytics can provide insights into whether current OKRs are advancing business success and where gaps may exist. Teams can then decide where to focus their efforts.

○ For instance, if a key result is **"Increase weekly active users by 10%,"** product managers can monitor user behavior trends using analytics platforms. If the product falls short, they can adjust marketing or feature development strategies to drive higher usage.

Example Interview Question:
"Describe a situation in which you had to ensure your product's OKRs (objectives and key results) aligned with the company's business goals. What did you do, and how did it turn out?"

Example Answer:

"At my previous company, the strategic objective was to increase market share within the enterprise segment. Our leadership set an objective for the product team: **'Expand our product suite to serve enterprise customer needs.'** The key results supporting this objective were: **'Develop and ship two new features focused on security compliance by Q3'** and **'Achieve a 20% increase in enterprise accounts.'** To ensure alignment, I facilitated cross-functional workshops with sales, marketing, and engineering teams to define the customer needs of the target market and our strategic focus. We established regular check-ins to monitor progress and adjusted when early feedback showed that one feature was not resonating as expected. By the end of the quarter, we successfully shipped both features and exceeded our target, achieving a 25% increase in enterprise accounts."

Importance of Aligning Product Teams with Business Goals

All companies, regardless of size or maturity, share a common goal: to create value for both stakeholders and customers. It is the interpretation and execution of this goal that defines a company's strategy and approach. The larger the company, the more distributed its employee base and the more complex these strategies and approaches become. Note that this complexity can exist within companies of any size, but many smaller companies either skirt the issue or fight the complexity directly and build governance structures that minimize negative impacts, thereby allowing their common goals to be better shared and staff empowered accordingly. The more complex the organization, the more necessary clear and direct messaging becomes. Messaging often becomes more opaque or bureaucratic as organizations grow or break into smaller competing or overlapping units.

5.7 Strategies for Aligning OKRs with Broader Business Objectives

Clear Communication and Transparency

Shared and commonly accessible goal-setting and management processes allow individuals to review and align their own goals, contributing to more holistic company-wide objectives. By helping your employees understand how their goals contribute to broader company-wide objectives, you empower them to take more responsibility for driving impact that contributes to overall company success.

An interview question that could help to discern the extent to which a candidate grasps the importance of clear communication, transparency, and mutual, goal-driven accountability in an OKR framework might be:

Example question: "Describe a time when you helped to ensure that a team's individual goals were aligned with broader organizational goals. What did you do to maintain open communication and transparency throughout the process?"

Good Response: "Prior to this, I led a cross-functional team that was responsible for introducing a new product feature. Before launching, I called an early kickoff meeting where I outlined the main goal and how that connected with the company's broader strategic goals. I then worked with each team member to set individual OKRs in support of that main goal—making sure everyone was aware of how their tasks contributed to the bigger picture.

This way, everyone could see how they were doing on their action items, and how that affected the larger timeline of the project. I also scheduled weekly check-ins so that we could address any open questions, give each other feedback, and adjust goals as needed, as well as celebrate milestones. This system not only kept people aligned, it also empowered them in their work, because they literally knew how their work made a difference."

Explanation: This response demonstrates a clear goal-setting ability, communication of goals, and a commitment to transparency. It shows the candidate to be a proactive leader, organized, and familiar with the OKR process through their focus on keeping the team aligned, communicating regularly regarding progress, and ensuring the process is accountable.

Cascading OKRs Throughout the Organization

In a strong company, cascading is a process by which top-level company objectives are gradually broken down into specific key results for each department, team and individual. The benefit of this approach is that every person in the organisation is able to see how they can contribute to the company's goals and ensure their work stays aligned to the strategic priorities of the organisation. For example, imagine that your company's CEO has set the following corporate OKRs:

OKR 1: Grow our market presence

OKR 2: Increase our customer base

OKR 3: Improve our sales process

The next step would be to break these corporate OKRs down into departmental objectives. The CEO and each department head would then work with their team leads to further break company OKRs into relevant and specific key results for each department. At the end of this step, each department would have clear objectives that cascade down from the corporate level.

Regular Review and Adjustment

Regular reviews keep the organisation calibrated on progress toward key outcomes of the company Regular reviews that establish a disciplined cadence are intrinsic to the OKR implementation process: for example, on a weekly basis, short-term progress is reviewed in weekly operational meetings; on a monthly basis, OKR progress is assessed in review meetings; and on a quarterly basis, strategic planning takes place to recalibrate or adjust OKRs at the beginning of each quarter. Such regular touchpoints ensure that teams keep focused, take corrective action in the event of a blocker, and, most importantly, adjust strategy when market dynamics or organisational priorities shift. Weekly, teams should be assessing key results in their various projects and identifying data trends to make adjustments, if needed; similarly, monthly reviews should allow a discussion of the same key results and data trends. Regular adjustments down the line prevent misalignment from growing into a larger problem, and keep teams across levels of the organisation focused on the outcomes that drive the company forward, reinforcing a culture of agility and experimentation.

Leveraging Technology for Alignment

Technology is essential to streamline the OKR process, to help more people and more parts of the organisation to be clear on the same objectives, and to provide full visibility into progress at every stage along the way. OKR management software gives companies a way to set, track and adjust goals in a single system that everyone can see, so goals are better aligned and visible to all employees. The platform allows team members to see how their work contributes to departmental and corporate goals, making it easier to diagnose issues of alignment early. And customised automation features save time and avoid manual errors with things such as goal-tracking in real time, data collection and performance analysis. Integrating OKR software with other tools such as project management systems, CRM or data analytics systems gives teams a 360-degree view of how work is progressing against strategic goals. This may reveal trends that require more attention or context. Technology creates a culture of accountability, collaboration and data-driven behaviour.

Overcoming Challenges in OKR Implementation

 OKRs can also be difficult to implement, especially in organisations that are new to the process. Some common challenges are setting objectives that are too ambitious or ambiguous, keeping goals clear during implementation, and ensuring alignment across different levels of the organisation. To overcome these challenges, it's important to start with clear and specific objectives. They need to be ambitious yet achievable, and each key result needs to be measurable, time-bound and directly linked to the objective. Leaders should listen to teams while they establish the goals and explain why something is an objective to foster greater buy-in and motivation. It's also critical to build regular check-ins where teams can review their progress and provide feedback on their OKRs. If it's not working, they can discuss how to adjust. Providing training on OKR best practices and supplying supportive tools for the process can also make this shift smoother.

Common OKR Pitfalls and How to Avoid Them

 Setting OKRs is not easy. To see, just look at how many organisations fall into the same traps that undermine their use.All companies who use OKRs or any other goal setting mechanism, will face issues at some point along the way. How the organisations respond to these issues will often be the measure of a successful team and product.

Among the most common pitfalls, we note:

Fuzzy Level-One Objectives: Lacking crisp, well-defined, and specific high-level objectives, there's no way to produce meaningful, aligned OKRs. Make sure company-wide objectives are crisp, well-defined and communicated to all employees.

31

Lacking here means teams will not be aligned and will waste efforts on items that do not fulfill the main goals of the company mission.

Lack of Employee Connection to the Mission: If employees don't understand how their individual goals relate to the wider mission, they might be lacklustre. Ask managers to articulate the strategic vision and how each OKR contributes to that vision. Easily this can lead to demotivation and wasted energy by team members as they scramble to find the right area to focus on.

Misalignment Between Departments: When teams create OKRs in silos, they may inadvertently state priorities and resource allocations that are not aligned with other departments. Having cross-functional teams work together on the goal-setting process helps avoid this.

Too Many OKRs: Setting too many OKRs can lead to burnout and dilution of focus. Make sure each team or person is only working on a few objectives so they can stay focused on what is most important. To avoid these mistakes, organisations must ensure that there is clear communication, structured planning and regular training that gives employees a common understanding of how to use OKRs to maximise performance and strategic success.

Addressing Misalignment Between OKRs and Business Goals

A mismatch between OKRs and the business objectives can severely impair an organisation's capability to execute its strategy. This section lists essential steps to ensure that OKRs are aligned with strategic objectives of the company:

Begin with a Clear Vision: First, define the company's long-term vision and strategic priorities. Capture and communicate them to all teams. All OKRs should be a step along the path to that vision.

Collaborate Across Teams: Encourage departmental collaboration during the goal-setting process to discourage unhelpful or unplanned competition. Cross-departmental workshops can both get everyone on the same page and ensure that OKRs don't end up in conflict with each other.

Revisit and revise OKRs regularly: Business priorities can shift rapidly and rigid OKRs can become obsolete. Check OKRs regularly and pivot or revise them as needed.

Use Data to Manage Alignment: Track progress against strategic objectives using data analytics, so that leaders know which teams are excelling, and can spot early signs of where teams are out of alignment.

Maintain Alignment Through Communication: Keeping teams aligned requires constant communication. Keep them well-informed about company priorities, progress towards critical objectives and changes in the strategic plan so that they all understand their part in the organisation.

By using these steps, we can create organisations that are sure to address misalignment, allowing all levels of the organisation to work towards the same goal.

Example Question: "Can you give me an example of what you would do if there were some misaligned goals within the company?"

Example Response: "In my previous company, we once had an issue where some of the team's OKRs were not 100 per cent linked to the company's strategic objectives. For example, when the company was trying to focus on customer retention, some of the teams were focusing heavily on the OKRs for new customer acquisition. I figured out this misalignment during the quarterly review.

To tackle this, I held a meeting in which we revisited the company's top-level goals and discussed how each team's OKRs could map back directly to those goals. I encouraged team leads to refine their OKRs so that they were aligned with the broader goal of customer retention. We also used an OKR tracking tool where everyone could see how their OKRs were mapped to the company's strategic objectives, which made any misalignment more apparent.

In addition, I instituted regular cadences and check-ins, accompanied by feedback loops that allowed teams to tweak their OKRs if needed (given shifts in the company strategy). This not only helped correct course but also fostered on-going, clear communication between teams, as well as a culture of alignment and shared goals."

Explanation: This response displays the ability to identify misalignment early on and address it through effective communication and collaboration, utilising technology to maintain transparency, constantly adjusting goals to reflect changes in the environment, and creating a feedback loop to keep the team focused on a common outcome. The answer also demonstrates leadership, problem-solving and a deep understanding of OKRs.

5.8 Interview tips for discussing goal setting and OKRs

You need to be able to demonstrate your ability to be a leader withing the organisation and help lead teams to success. Your role of Product Manager is to support your tech teams to align with the organisation.

These are the skills employers are looking for in this current wave of Product Management. More than ever the Product Manager is asked to lead and set the pace and tone as well as strategy for the organisation. While not solely responsible for these areas, the Product Manager at any level needs to be able to demonstrate their ability to be a leader within this area.

Good to keep in mind this small framework when tackling questions related to goal setting and OKRs:

Comprehension: Demonstrate familiarity with OKRs as a method of establishing goals that connect individual objectives to company targets.

Utilization: Discuss how you applied OKRs to set precise, measurable goals and monitor progress.

Flexibility: Showcase instances where you adapted OKRs in response to new information, demonstrating your capacity to shift focus while staying aligned with strategy.

Teamwork: Highlight your ability to collaborate across departments to secure team agreement and dedication to mutual OKRs.

The team that is hiring you do not have all the answers and they do not expect you to have them all either. But you need to prove you can hold your own in the process of goal development and execution as this is ultimately how we plan to deliver value within the organisation.

Chapter 6: Product Strategy & Vision

6.1. Introduction to Product Strategy & Vision and What Interviewers Are Looking for in a Product Manager

One of the critical roles of product management is to lead the definition and articulation of the product strategy and vision. This vision outlines the broad goals for the product and communicates the organization's desired future state. This aligned view of the future clarifies and regularizes decision-making and prioritization. Effective visions thus provide all relevant stakeholders with a common reference point and an understanding of why they are working towards the product's goals. When evaluating candidates for product manager positions, many interviewers use this critical role as an indicator of candidate preparation for the role.

Effective product managers align their large and small-scale responsibilities to their vision to create the most value for the organization while facilitating strategy execution. As such, hiring managers frequently look at the candidates' ability to understand and communicate product strategy and how it exemplifies their current or past work. Multiple sources detail the competencies needed to be an effective product manager. While some of these competencies differ slightly in naming or scope, they share core areas of focus. Whether formally listed or implied, the majority of product management competencies directly or indirectly reference good strategic vision or its alignment with executing strategy. Candidates can capitalize on this information during job interviews, as articulating product strategy effectively can significantly influence hiring decisions.

User engagement has been described as one of the principal cornerstones of successful product strategies. Stating that increased user engagement is a critical outcome of the product strategy shows a commitment to improving overall business value. Another cornerstone is clearly linking product development stakes within a well-crafted product vision. Candidates for product manager roles are expected to demonstrate a profound understanding of the importance of, and provide quantifiable evidence supporting, their product vision. Based on their portfolio or others' work, the quality of a candidate's product strategy and vision can be fairly readily extrapolated from interview data.

6.2. Importance of Long-Term Product Vision in Interviews

Having a long-term vision for a product and being able to articulate it is a great way to stand out in interviews for product manager roles. Interviewers often use these questions to differentiate candidates. Strong candidates can accurately identify trends in the field and articulate a strategic direction their product could take advantage of or contribute to. It's helpful for this 'vision' to be aspirational, but what really impresses the interviewer is evidence of strategic thinking. Candidates with a clear vision that aligns with market trends make the best impression.

Interviews for product manager positions typically include a discussion about long-term product vision. A great product vision can instill confidence among internal and external stakeholders, like team members, business partners, and consultants. When rendering the product strategy, the vision should provide proper insights and develop trust among stakeholders. A great product vision combines creativity with thorough market examination. It should be aspirational yet grounded in market trends, showing a basic understanding of the industry.

6.3. Aligning Product Roadmap with Company Objectives

The product roadmap must align with company objectives and the strategy the company wants to follow. Product managers need to design a roadmap that reflects the company's strategic goals and communicates the importance of their strategy. Various tools or frameworks, such as the Objectives and Key Results (OKR) framework, help companies communicate strategy effectively and ensure that PMs align their products with it.

If the product vision is central, and the company has feedback loops integrating the product into its strategy, the roadmap aligns with company goals. Interviews then focus on evaluating PMs' abilities to think about and discuss potential futures and product positioning. Candidates who can identify such a roadmap strategy in their past roles may be asked to explain how it aligned with the company's vision and what successes resulted. Providing a case study demonstrates how company buy-in occurred and how product success contributed to business results.

6.4. Proving Competencies Based on Seniority Level

The expectation of competencies for product management roles varies based on seniority:

- **Entry-Level:** For entry-level candidates, the focus is less on hands-on product experience and more on proving they have researched the role and understand why it fits them. Competencies target skills such as critical thinking, leadership potential, and intelligence. Discussing transferable skills, such as project management and research, can help compensate for inexperience.
- **Senior Product Manager/Principal Product Manager:** Candidates are expected to demonstrate substantial product management experience and leadership ability, possibly having served as a head of or VP of product. Examples should highlight

extensive leadership experiences, including hiring and building teams. At this level, discussing teamwork alongside other critical abilities is crucial.

- **Executives (VP or C-suite roles):** Candidates for executive roles must showcase an extensive background in product leadership and the ability to discuss this in detail, including their impact and influence within past organizations.

Chapter 7: Managing and Leading Through Change and Uncertainty

In today's fast-paced world of short-term business objectives, change is the norm, and uncertainty often becomes the new status quo. When companies face challenges from market shifts, rapid technological evolution, or internal restructuring, effective product managers don't just cope with change—they drive it. As anchors for their teams, they ensure everyone is in sync, sees things the same way, and moves with a unified vision. Successful change management requires a clear understanding of why change is necessary, effective communication, and the confidence to manage (and anticipate) uncertainty. This chapter will identify key strategies to help you lead through change, manage uncertainty, and build and sustain resilience in your teams, ensuring success even amid the turbulence.

7.1. Building Change-Ready Teams

The first step to effective change management is fostering an organizational culture where flexibility, resilience, and openness to new ideas prevail. Here are some key strategies:

1. **Cultivate an Adaptive Culture**: Make change a norm, not an aberration. Teams accustomed to change are less resistant and more likely to view it as a springboard for innovation. Encourage constant learning, experimentation, and openness to new approaches and technologies. The more change becomes embedded in the business culture, the more your team will proactively seek it to gain a competitive edge.
2. **Explain the 'Why'**: Clearly articulate the need for change and what it aims to accomplish. Is there a market shift that requires a response? Are customer needs evolving? Could internal processes be improved? Connecting the change to the

organization's broader strategy helps build support and reduces uncertainty.
3. **Engage Stakeholders Early and Often**: Change impacts everyone, not just the product team. Engaging with stakeholders (executives, marketing, engineering, sales, customers) early ensures visibility, co-creation, and ownership over the change. It also uncovers potential resistance points, allowing for proactive management.
4. **Provide Training and Support**: Equip teams with the knowledge and tools they need to navigate new processes, tools, or approaches. Training sessions, workshops, and resources prepare team members to step up when faced with new challenges, fostering a sense of readiness and confidence.
5. **Measure Progress and Pivot**: Establish metrics to track success. Monitor performance, listen to feedback, and be willing to adapt if plans don't unfold as expected. Flexibility and responsiveness foster a culture of learning where teams feel empowered to experiment and iterate.

7.2. Demonstrating Change Management Skills in Interviews

Employers seek product managers who can guide teams through periods of ambiguity with a calm, strategic approach. When discussing your experiences, emphasize the following qualities:

1. **Vision and Agility**: Demonstrate how you've led teams through change by setting a clear vision and shifting course when necessary. Employers value candidates who can maintain long-term focus while adapting to immediate challenges. Flexibility allows you to keep a steady hand on the wheel, even on a rollercoaster of change.
2. **Case-Based Leadership Examples**: Use concrete examples to showcase your leadership. Describe specific scenarios where you navigated change, such as managing a market shift, implementing a new workflow, or pivoting a product direction. Explain what you did, why you did it, how you kept people engaged, and the outcomes of your leadership.

3. **Collaboration and Communication**: Effective change management requires clear stakeholder communication. Describe how you kept stakeholders informed, managed expectations, and ensured alignment around the shared vision. Mention any frameworks or methodologies you used to smooth the transition.
4. **Agile Decision Making**: Employers appreciate quick, decisive action in the face of ambiguity. Share examples of how you've navigated uncertain situations, using tools like risk analysis, SWOT analysis, or decision trees. Explain how your ability to prioritize and make strategic decisions positively impacted your projects and teams.
5. **Emotional Intelligence and Empathy**: Change can be stressful, and people often react on an emotional level. Highlight how you've supported your team by listening to their concerns, providing a safe space for discussion, and offering programs or activities to help them adapt.

7.3. Strategies for Leading Teams Through Uncertain Times

Leading teams successfully through turbulent and volatile conditions requires strategic forethought, flexibility, and empathy. Here are effective strategies to employ:

1. **Scenario Planning**: Prepare for future outcomes by developing contingency plans. Predict potential challenges and create backup plans to ensure your team can continue moving forward. Show how you've used scenario planning to anticipate issues and adapt quickly when unexpected changes occur.
2. **Empower Your Teams**: Give team members autonomy to make decisions within their areas of expertise. Empowerment fosters a sense of ownership and accountability, crucial in unpredictable environments. When team members feel trusted, they're more likely to develop innovative solutions and proactively address problems.
3. **Regular Check-Ins and Feedback Loops**: Maintain open communication through regular check-ins. Use these opportunities to gather feedback, address concerns, and adjust strategies.

Continuous dialogue keeps teams aligned and responsive, making it easier to detect and resolve potential disruptions in real-time.

4. **Risk Management**: Develop a comprehensive approach to anticipating risks before they become problems. Explain how you create an inventory of potential risks, develop mitigation strategies, and communicate these strategies to the team. Risk management is about readiness to act quickly when issues arise.

7.4. Conflict Management During Change

Change can often lead to conflict as teams adapt to new ways of working. Managing conflict effectively is essential for any product manager. Consider these strategies:

1. **Signs of Conflict**: Learn to recognize early indications of conflict. Are team members engaging in heated discussions, or withdrawing into silence? Act quickly to explore and address underlying issues before they escalate.
2. **Facilitation and Mediation**: Use facilitation skills to bring stakeholders together around shared problems. Maintain a respectful space that allows dissent but ensures all voices are heard.
3. **Turning Conflict Into Collaboration**: Frame conflict as a source of creativity. Disagreements can lead to innovative solutions. Show how you've used conflict to build buy-in and foster collaboration, showcasing your ability to leverage diverse perspectives.
4. **Transparency and Consistency**: Be transparent about changes and consistent in enforcing new processes. Building trust helps prevent resistance, as team members will see that everyone is treated equally. Trust is key to effective change management and conflict resolution.

7.5. Metrics for Success: Evaluating Change Management Efforts

Measuring the impact of change management initiatives is challenging but essential. Here's what you should track:

1. **Time-to-Adaptation**: Measure how quickly your team adopts new processes. Faster adaptation indicates effective communication, training, and support structures.
2. **Stakeholder Satisfaction**: Collect feedback on how well the change was managed. High satisfaction scores indicate strong leadership, collaboration, and communication.
3. **Performance Indicators**: Track performance metrics before and after changes. Improved metrics, such as reduced product defects, faster development cycles, or increased productivity, demonstrate successful change management.
4. **Cost-Benefit Analysis**: Assess the financial impact of change initiatives. Did strategies lead to cost savings, increased revenue, or better resource allocation? Use data to back your findings and show how effective change management contributes to the bottom line.

7.6. Key Takeaways for PM Interviews

When discussing your change management experience in interviews, focus on the following:

1. **Point Flexibility**: Show that you can adapt to changing circumstances while maintaining long-term focus.
2. **Illustrate Leadership**: Use examples to demonstrate how you led teams through change, showing both strategic decisions and daily leadership actions.
3. **Quantify Outcomes**: Provide data to illustrate the benefits of your efforts—faster turnaround, happier customers, or reduced costs.
4. **Show Emotional Intelligence**: Describe how you supported team members during difficult periods, building trust, resilience, and fostering collaboration.

If you master these skills, you'll become a leader capable of guiding teams through uncertainty, making you an indispensable asset in today's fluid tech world.

8. Product-Led Growth in Product Manager Interviews

8.1. Introduction to Product-Led Growth (PLG)

Product-Led Growth (PLG) is a go-to-market approach that employs a product's core value proposition as a unifying framework across the whole organization: driving adoption toward end users, with the value of the company's offering resting in the product, shifting the company's growth engine away from the sales team and into the product itself.

PLG principles can be summarized into three key points:

- The product takes the user experience as its primary acquisition, expansion, and retention funnel.
- It advocates for no-touch user experiences delivered through the product itself.
- Acquisition, expansion, and retention focus on individual user-led adoption.

Information technology developed in such a way that product-led growth has not only become possible but also made a desire for intuitive and user-friendly products a core part of the customer experience. **Customer acquisition, product management, customer success** and other areas have been affected by PLG, leading to reduced costs and better customer retention.

8.2. Evaluation of Product-Led Growth in Interviews

In interviews, PLG knowhow is probed both theoretically and in terms of lived experience. The interviewer should discern the candidate's familiarity with PLG concepts, strategies, and real-world examples by asking questions such as:

- Experience in implementing PLG strategies or opting for sales-led growth.
- Examples of using models like freemium to drive growth.
- Insights gained from user interactions and data in the context of PLG.

8.2.1. Importance of PLG in Product Manager Roles

PLG lets product managers allocate resources to features that meet users' needs more profitably. This leads to better product-market fit, a 'virtuous circle' between how the product is developed and how it fuels growth, and the use of data (e.g., feature uptake during the trial stage and post-trial retention) to refine strategies and innovate.

Highlighting the importance of **frictionless onboarding**, **user feedback**, and **feature adoption** elevates retention and accelerates scaling. PLG strategies give organizations a competitive edge; the organizational power of PMs is harnessed to further their businesses by the practice of PLG.

8.3. Strategies to Demonstrate PLG in Interviews

Demonstrating PLG knowledge in case studies involves:

- **Documenting Your Experience**: Write down stories about times when you applied PLG – for example, when you made it easier for users to adopt the product, or when you asked customers what motivated or confused them about your product. Then, note the business impact and the actions you took.
- **Storytelling**: Tell your impact story in a structured narrative which outlines the problem, the solution, and the results in numbers. Show your successes, failures, changes, and assess how you adapted and led through them.
- **Demonstrating Success**: Pick examples that relate to the company's goals and metrics. Link what you did to the product or business results, and show your strategic thinking and execution.

When discussing PLG implementation:

- Describe the stories of PLG initiatives that you have led or played an integral part in, illuminating the strategic trade-offs you made along the way and their role in driving business results.
- Tie them back to **business value**: growth metrics, customer retention, and improvements in product agility through PLG strategies.
- Show thoughtfulness by articulating key future plans for PLG or specific features that support long-term business objectives. Back up the plan with success proof points, challenges, and lessons learned.

8.4. Optimizing the Business Model in a PLG Framework

Mastery of Product-Led Growth (PLG) strategy goes beyond user acquisition – a strong PLG strategy also means business models that drive revenue through multiple channels. Product managers should be able to speak to how they've optimized business models through tactics such as freemiums, upsells, cross-sells, and enabling sales.

Freemium as a Hook: Free is a key element of PLG. In general, freemium means users get basic features of a core product for free, with paid upgrades on top. Explain how you've balanced giving enough value in the free tier to encourage user adoption while keeping the path to upgrades clear. Describe how you designed a freemium approach to facilitate the greatest conversion without making the upgrades aggressive or opaque.

Upsell and Cross-Sell Opportunities: The importance of upselling and cross-selling to a PLG model cannot be understated, so product managers must develop a strong understanding of what opportunities exist in the user journey to introduce premium features or other products. As you prep for interviews, think about how you leveraged data to identify high-value users, how you customized upsells based on user behavior, and what value propositions you used to communicate the ongoing value of additional features or services in a way that drove conversion.

Enhancing the Sales Team With PLG Insights: No matter how PLG-driven an organization is, many enterprises with high-value customers require account executives as part of the sales process. Product managers can help the sales team in multiple ways with data insights picked up from usage of the product: highlight qualified leads (e.g., the product could have automatically captured free-trial signups that used all features for 30 days or more), show who the most engaged users are, share with sales your metrics on Product Qualified Leads (PQLs), and share usage patterns that distinguish the most engaged users from those who merely dabble with the product. In interviews, talk about how you've helped accelerate and improve the sales process with actionable insights from user data. Talk about how those insights have led to business results.

Value-Driven Features: Monetization isn't just about freemium and upsells. It's also about designing and launching value-driven features that match your users' needs and enable more revenue. Talk about feature gaps you've identified, premium offerings you've built, and user feedback that helped to guide you in building valuable product roadmaps for both user growth and monetization.

48

Maximizing Customer Lifetime Value (CLTV): Another key element of business model optimization is focusing on retention and maximizing the lifetime value of the customers. Retention is often much cheaper than acquisition, and PLG strategies should include tactics for driving longer-term engagement and loyalty. Provide examples of how you've driven CLTV through customer success programs, further value communication, and feature enhancements based on user data.

8.5. Key PLG Metrics and KPIs

Following a PLG framework, tracking success for a product means looking at specific numbers that show product adoption and company growth. When interviewing for a product management position, get ready to talk about the following metrics and how you've used them to optimize your PLG strategies:

- **User Engagement Rates**: The DAU/MAU (daily/monthly active users) measure shows the level of engagement and how well the product retains users.
- **Customer Acquisition Costs (CAC)**: How much does it cost to acquire new customers? In a PLG model, lower CAC often stems from the self-service nature of acquisition.
- **Customer Lifetime Value (CLTV)**: A measure of the entire future value of a customer relationship. Maximizing CLTV is fundamental to profitability over time.
- **Product-Qualified Leads (PQLs)**: PQLs are users for whom your product demonstrated enough value to convert them into paying customers. Share how you take your PQLs from free to paid.
- **Churn Rate**: Tracking churn monitors when users leave and why, enabling product managers to adjust strategies and prevent user loss.

With knowledge of these metrics and when to use them, product managers can help fine-tune PLG, as well as show users and the organization where value grows.

8.6. PLG and Cross-Functional Collaboration

PLG isn't just the responsibility of the product team. It cuts across departments, from marketing and sales to customer success and engineering. Demonstrate how you have worked with cross-functional teams, how you've helped them align on product goals, thought through user experience, and drove growth.

Marketing Cooperation: Outline where you have worked closely with marketing to perfect messaging around the product, test onboarding flows and experiments to increase adoption, or leverage feedback from the customer success teams to deliver better and more engaging experiences across the journey.

Engineering and Design Collaboration: Show where you've worked with engineering and design teams to offer better user experiences and drive higher levels of engagement by building and designing the product in sync with user needs and expectations.

Effective cross-functional collaboration is crucial to ensuring that PLG strategies are executed well, and that all organizational teams are aligned in goal pursuit.

8.7. Challenges in Implementing PLG

Though PLG promises many advantages, it can also present many challenges. Be prepared to answer questions about the difficulties you encountered and how you overcame them – for example:

- **Rationing Resources**: Growth-oriented strategies can strain scarce resources. Outline your approach for prioritizing ROI-maximizing initiatives without taxing your team.
- **Fighting Feature Creep**: Feature creep is a concern for PLG, and PMs must navigate high-ROI features to avoid feature bloat while still delivering value to drive adoption.

- **Over-Relying on Product-Led Growth**: PLG isn't a solution for every business challenge. Explain how you balanced product-led efforts with customer support and other avenues of growth to ensure a comprehensive approach.

By discussing these challenges and how you handled them, you demonstrate your appreciation for the broader picture of PLG and how different roles interconnect.

8.8. The Role of Data in PLG

Data-driven decision-making is critical to PLG. Product managers are reliant on data and analytics to make changes and optimize the user experience, increase adoption, and improve customer retention. When interviewing, talk about how you've used data to:

- **Track User Behavior**: Understand friction points, feature usage, and opportunities for improvement.
- **Inform Product Decisions**: Use the data to prioritize product features that will provide the most value to the most users (and thus drive the most business results).
- **Iterate on PLG Strategies**: Test, learn, and iterate to continuously improve product-led strategies.

8.9. PLG in B2B vs. B2C

B2B and B2C PLG strategies can be quite different, and product managers should be able to discuss these differences in interviews. In B2B contexts, the sales cycle is often longer, with more stakeholders involved before closing a deal. B2B PLG can often be a hybrid model, where the product drives adoption, but sales teams still play a role in converting larger accounts. In B2C contexts, PLG is often faster, with viral growth and social proof playing significant roles.

If relevant, ensure your interview answers detail how you've tailored PLG strategies for B2B and B2C contexts, including key differences in user engagement, adoption, and how customer feedback is integrated into each model.

Being a product person that can work in both b2c and b2b is a great asset. It is highly encouraged for the reader to pursue both areas and then perhaps specialise in one area if needed. The market also oscillates between startups being usually in waves of B2B or B2C focused, so being able to show proficiency in both areas is always handy.

Chapter 9: Tackling Product Discovery in Product Management Interviews

9.1. Understanding Product Discovery tracks

Product discovery is the second of the three phases of product management. This phase is where the magic happens and products start taking shape. Discovery is about finding out what should be built in the most rigorous and systematic way possible, so that you provide a product that user wants and will use. This phase helps product managers, designers and engineers be good at understanding users, problem and solution. Discovery enables them to find the right problems and solve them in the best possible way.

Expect to be probed on your understanding of product discovery in interviews. The company wants to know if you can develop the workflow that takes a product concept from idea to validation. You'll need to answer questions like these during product discovery:

Who are the users?

What are their needs?

What problems are they facing?

What are the potential solutions?

And product discovery, the early work involved with identifying a product idea, involves such things as user interviews, market research, prototyping and usability testing. Without getting early feedback, it's easier for product managers to wind up building something completely useless, ultimately wasting the time and money of the product team. You need to pay attention to qualitative insights, but you also need to pay attention to quantitative data – to empathy and to rigour You are also asked to function at the intersection of governance and entrepreneurship.

A product discovery process in an agile, fast environment is highly iterative. The PM is the person in the room consistently evaluating market price/conditions, consumer need, and product feasibility – and orchestrating working groups including business, design, engineering, data science, etc – all in a process that has to move at a fierce pace. A key part of the PM's role is not just filtering ideas; it's also knowing when to kill an idea. That rapid killing is key to good product managers who can drive the right work through a hyper-productive team.

Interview Question:

"How do you prioritize features during the discovery phase?"

Example Answer:

"I rely on qualitative and quantitative data when considering what features to prioritise in the short-term. For instance, on a B2B SaaS product I worked on, we would frequently conduct user interviews and surveys to get feedback on features that were most important to users for that particular week. We would then combine that with product analytics and look at features that users were using the most and the least, and where there were gaps and opportunities. On the trade-off between short-term and long-term, I would use frameworks like RICE (Reach, Impact, Confidence, Effort) to score features that came up. In one situation, we purposefully deprioritised a high-effort feature that had a low impact on the user experience. Instead, we focused on improving core functionality and saw a 15 per cent reduction in customer churn."

9.2. Understanding Product Deliverability

Delivery follows discovery as the time to make it real, focusing on turning insights and hypotheses into meaningful experiences for users. Delivery is the point at which teams switch their energy from learning and exploring to executing towards a clear, distinctive vision.

Within this, product delivery is really about handling the end-to-end lifecycle of the product output – not the tactical details, but being able to coordinate cross-functional teams to have a shared vision of what success looks like and when it is going to happen. Once everyone is aligned, it's about making sure that the product is built, released when it needs to be, and is high quality. A product manager helps to communicate, removes blockers, and makes sure people are focused on achieving the goal.

Agile methodologies, scrum frameworks and continuous integration/continuous deployment (CI/CD) are critical components to this phase. PMs must not only have a command of these processes, but understand how to adapt them to the needs of their team and project. Responsibilities here include:

Tracking progress and managing project timelines.

Addressing any risks, dependencies, or scope creep.

Conducting user testing and quality assurance (QA) before launching the product.

Feedback loops are also part of the continuous testing during delivery to make sure the product meets user needs, even as it gets closer and closer to being complete. Delivery success relies heavily on wellstructured ceremonies and processes, such as backlog grooming, sprint planning and release planning, to keep teams focused on what needs to be completed and when.

9.3. Mastering the Balance Between Product Discovery and Delivery in Interviews

One of the key differentiators for any product manager is the ability to navigate the art and science of product discovery vs product delivery. These two phases of the product lifecycle require very distinct mindsets, skill sets, and strategies – yet both are equally critical to executing on a product vision successfully. Being able to seamlessly traverse both phases, and validate that you can thrive in both, is a common interview challenge in product management.

In Product **Discovery**, you're the one who is exploring opportunities, lowering uncertainty and gathering insights to steer the product's direction. You'll want to show that you can conduct user research, synthesise feedback and apply strategic thinking to prioritising product features. Also that you can lead the cross-functional team in brainstorming solutions, validating ideas and iterating on product designs.

In Product **Delivery**, you refocus on execution – bringing all those validated insights together to deliver tangible outputs. People who get hired into this role are tasked with delivering on promises, keeping teams aligned, and managing cost, timelines and risks to deliver a product to market. You get ahead in this phase by first mastering the execution game – minimising the branching complexity that can derail a product that doesn't meet its goals or business objectives.

Demonstrate that you can expertly both handle discovery and delivery – and motion from one to the other – is a powerful way to demonstrate what you bring to the table in an interview. How discovery informed delivery, and vice-versa. For example, how was your initial thinking from discovery used in informing your product strategy? How were the insights from discovery used in making sure that the product was successfully delivered?

Furthermore, describe how you've learned to recover from times when one process became too dominant at the expense of the other. How did you shift gears if delivery began before enough discovery work had been done, or when discovery went on for too long and delayed the execution process?

Key Interview Questions You May Encounter:

Describe a scenario in which you exhibited product discovery leadership: How did you provide leadership to design, product management, data science, market research and engineering? How did you leverage data at each stage?What were your key insights, and how did these insights impact the decisions that you made?

What do you do to take a product discovery team and flow that information through delivery? Once you have come up with the initial concept for an item that your company wants to build, how do you make sure the process doesn't lose steam along the way?

What approaches do you take to tether product discovery to product delivery – to make sure the team is on the same page and solving the right problem?

Best Practices for Framing Your Interview Answers:

To demonstrate how discovery informs delivery, weave answers to highlight how the work completed in discovery impacted delivery. For example, explain how the early validation of product features in discovery de-risked delivery and improved the ability to execute.

Tie Discovery to Business Outcomes: Demonstrate how the insights generated in discovery were connected back to company objectives and met the needs of the customers. Show how delivering against these insights helped the organisation derive measurable value.

Demonstrate a Collaborative Approach: If possible, demonstrate your ability to lead cross-functional teams through both Product phases. Describe how you helped to align stakeholders' communication and priorities into a unified product vision.

9.4. Pitfalls to Avoid in Balancing Discovery and Delivery

Finally, there are common pitfalls to avoid in interviews as well, in terms of the balance between discovery and delivery:

Overemphasising Delivery Without Discovery: Building without a strong discovery phase can mean delivering the wrong product, or creating unnecessary features that users don't want or need. Be prepared to talk about how you sidestepped this issue by getting insights and data early on.

Staying in the Discovery phase too long: On the other hand, staying too long in the discovery phase can kill momentum and also delay time-to-market. Explain how you've been able to compress the discovery timeline without creating analysis paralysis and killing momentum.

Poor stakeholder alignment: Maybe you didn't communicate clearly when ideas were first being tested, or perhaps stakeholders took actions that misaligned the work from your original goals. Show how you made sure everyone involved was on board, all the way from the ideation stage to the delivery of the final product.

9.5. Measuring Success in Discovery and Delivery

Next, be clear on how you'd measure success: both during the discovery phase, and the delivery phase. In the interview, show an ability to track and measure KPIs for each of these phases. Some suggestions:

Discovery KPI: Customer feedback quality, number of validated features, time spent in discovery vs outcomes.

Delivery KPIs: Time-to-market, development velocity, sprint completion rate, and quality assurance metrics.

Having a perspective on what to measure for both discovery and delivery (what we call 'north stars' and 'sailboats', respectively) helps you understand how to handle the lifecycle of products and makes you a better product manager.

Chapter 10: The Role of Metrics and Analytical Thinking in Product Management Interviews

10.1. Introduction to Product Metrics

I can roughly group product management interviews that involve any amount of analytical thinking into two categories. The first has a tendency to ask questions that make you think about what kind of things a PM working on a specific problem would want to measure—these are product metrics questions. The second doesn't really care that much what you're measuring, but will instead give you a list of data and expect you to ask questions and draw conclusions based on this information. These are data analysis questions. The good news is that once you get good at product metrics, you can also answer these questions with some amount of confidence. This is why we prioritize product metrics in the week 1 curriculum. I'll also say that I've had friends get these kinds of questions at the same company with no warning—so this is important stuff.

A product metric is a specific quantitative measure of a product or feature that indicates how well the product or feature is doing on one or another axis. These can truly be of any order of complexity but fall into four broad buckets: Web Analytics, Funnel Metrics, User Metrics, and Economic Impact. While this question absolutely involves numbers, product metrics aren't always numbers. They're just ways of measuring movement in one way or another, so while there are definitely user count metrics, there are also subjective "feel" metrics, like head pain seconds. When you've gotten a little practice with coming up with what to measure, it becomes time to figure out how to measure product.

10.1.1. Understanding the Importance of Product Metrics

Metrics are one of the few ways to show the health of the product over time. If you grow or have positive value in some critical metrics, then the product is considered healthy; and if the metrics have negative traction, then chances are that the product growth opportunity is less. Product metrics are everywhere, from an onboarding funnel to customer satisfaction, and from the lifetime value of customers to how much it costs to acquire a new customer. It's one of the most used mechanisms to make informed product decisions in the product management lifecycle. The best part is that they can give you trends seen in the historical data and the opportunities to address for future planning.

Successful product managers are a blend of soft data (user feelings and behavior) and hard data. Metrics provide the kind of validation, through trends and values, that quantitatively driven professionals thrive on. Metrics, when they move in relation to each other, can indicate interesting things. For instance, if transaction volume per day is growing, but user count is capped, and the per-user metric is dropping, this means that customer satisfaction is dropping. It also means that we expect our future sales pipeline (and other operational metrics) to be adversely impacted by expired pre-pay subscriptions, more churn, and less upsell. In other words, metrics can inform our future product features. Hopefully, you appreciate the sorts of interesting things you can interpret out of converging or diverging metrics.

Finally, and most importantly, metrics indicate the answer to all worldly problems: where should you spend your time? The key to understanding data in PM interviews is not data itself; it is to tease out the justification behind it. That's why, in this guide, we start with an understanding of the underlying product metric and its rationale.

10.2. Presenting Your Approach to Product Metrics in Interviews

Most of your interviews contain a section where you get to present your approach to product metrics. Interviewers expect candidates to be familiar with common e-commerce, marketplace, SaaS, hardware/software, and other key product metrics, as well as capable of analyzing the results and backing up the rationale behind focusing on some metrics while deprioritizing others. While not a universal truth, product management interviews often follow a sequence: first, a generic recruiter interview, then another product manager or a product representative will follow, and it will be this person's task to evaluate your analytical thinking and metric knowledge. Given the first-round interview feedback and rejections, don't overcomplicate things; offer a structured, concise, yet sufficient response to exceed the interviewer's metric expectations. After discussing your high-level approach to product metrics, prepare yourself to tell a coherent story regarding your hands-on experience dealing with such metrics. Before the interview, research the company and team and tailor this response to the metrics you'll be responsible for in the organization. Research the material you need to prepare and, if the team you interview for hasn't already approached you for sample documents, build a couple of mock ones to share. If the decision differs from what you would usually take in the company, be confident in justifying why you took it. You may not have expertise with predictive modeling, but if the firm is way ahead of you in this aspect and the dataset is strong enough, feel free to indicate it.

10.3 Key Strategies for Communicating Your Metric Approach

This subsection dives into specific strategies for demonstrating your approach to using metrics in product management interviews. You should focus on being clear about the complexity that goes into defining a metric and remain concise in its discussion. Visuals help others digest information and may be used when you start describing a metric, with visuals accompanying you, as well as follow-up questions. Always bring your metrics back to a need or objective in context, such as customer or business needs. Also, keep in mind that metric questions could be part of your execution or technical loop, primarily for product managers, but sometimes for designers and tech leads, as well as your product design loop and/or systematic metrics hiring criteria. Expect follow-up questions about how you've used these metrics; be prepared to add or further explain two to three specific instances for each kind that you have worked with. Be prepared to discuss metrics from others' points of view as the target group, such as senior stakeholders, team members, and customers.

- **Preparation and Practice.** As with most things, success in these questions comes down to practice. The more you think through and practice talking about your thoughts on different metrics, the more comfortable you'll feel discussing metrics in the moment.
- **Anticipate Follow-Ups.** Have prepared examples from your recent career of a time you made a decision based on a metric and why you chose that metric.
- **Signal enthusiasm for data-driven approaches.** Convey enthusiasm and follow-through about using data to inform decisions and experiments. At the end of loop debrief meetings, signal that you are particularly excited about candidates who use data to drive experiments and decisions.

10.4. Data-Driven Decision-Making

A data-driven framework for making decisions led to a 5% higher improvement in customer satisfaction and a 4% higher increase in return on investment. Over 50% of the companies surveyed have seen a significant change in business outcomes after relying on data. Product managers must rely on a range of indicators to make the decisions that will shape a product's direction, improve it over time, and increase its chances of hitting established targets.

Those indicators are called metrics. A metric is a quantifiable data point used to measure progress and track the success of a business. The most successful product managers are those who are able to tie that data to solid analysis, perspective, and expertise.

This mindset can be practiced in the early days of product management, and if ethically applied, will enable you to lead products with ease. The origin of data can be varied, including, but not limited to, user feedback, competitor and market analysis, and the product and team's performance. A note on user feedback: not all feature requests are a good idea. Perhaps it is the reach of the request, or the importance of understanding the "real" problem that matters, but it is worth a mention when considering all sources of data. The sources are not absolutes. But again, when balanced with solid analysis, history, and a forward-looking view, product managers are better equipped to make plans that will then guide the direction of the product. Interpreting data is just as important in product management as identifying which data to collect. Using pretenses, biases, or misconceptions to view the "truth space" will either lead to an inaccurate (opinionated) session or a completely different result than anticipated.

10.4.1. The Significance of Data-Driven Decisions in Product Management

Product management is unique as it relies on data-driven analytical evidence throughout the product development cycle. The ability to collect, analyze, and make decisions based on data is crucial to its successful execution. Understanding the consumer and using data can result in improved response and product performance. The iterative nature of product development and the role data plays throughout the iterative stages is essential. Your venture is just a hypothesis, but it's the steps you take: hypothesis, test, learn, retest, etc. This is a continuous basis for incremental innovation.

The vision is all sexy and cool; ideas are a dime a dozen. The metric that matters most is whether your product gets to product-market fit. And measuring those top-line metrics that show the locomotion of your business gives you a clear idea of the iterative refinements you need to make. Using analytics is strongly applied in digital and online service companies, but is often mentioned as a challenge for product managers in B2B companies. The biggest challenge for product managers today is still spreading data and insight to get the organization to collaborate: how to achieve good cooperation and feedback loops throughout the company is the big challenge. Being able to do this requires commercial understanding and a common vision. It is crucial that the organization values the same. Providing awareness of those principles to marketing, engineering, designers, etc., is something that can make us a lot more effective and productive.

10.5. Expectations from Potential Product Manager Hires

Any organization is likely to expect a potential hire to understand metrics to the point of including another way to use them themselves, for instance, in their product management interviews. The exercise is about seeing how you think about and interpret data. They are seeing how you explain your reasoning and conclusions. They are seeing how you seek out relevant details in a huge sea of irrelevant details. They are seeing how well you can communicate a technical subject in corporate language. The interview process is also to gauge chemistry and make sure that the candidate has the right attitude and aptitude. Part of a PM's success is the efficacy with which they perform quantitative analysis. It is not for all organizations, but the hires can be expected to have at least an informed analytical background and mindset to talk about how they have conducted quantitative analysis in a past scenario. Candidates can also be expected to review a large collection of numbers and relevant data that have meaning with respect to the strategy of an organization. A few lines of inquiry could be: Product teams need to consider metrics on their product strategies—what are one or two things that could go right (or wrong) with using metrics to drive the product? How do people really think about metrics and data analysis in a practical, in-the-trenches kind of way?

10.6. What Interviewers Look for in Data-Driven Decision-Making Skills

The primary skills and attributes that interviewers are looking for when assessing a candidate's data-driven decision-making capabilities are somewhat overlapping with those sought when discussing vision. A lot of this boils down to how you can analyze information and demonstrate the final result or next steps.

- Analytical rigor and familiarity with using multiple types of product data and metrics to reach a conclusion.
- Ability to take incomplete data and create compelling, data-driven narratives.
- Being able to take this information and make a conclusion usually boils down to communication and succinct summation of the points.
- Strong communication skills to convey findings and results clearly.
- Being able to explain technical or data-heavy work to someone who is likely not a product manager and could be mid-level in another area.
- Examples of things you've learned or insights you've gained from looking at data.
- Examples of how this has either forced you to adapt your decision-making or resulted in notable success.
- Ways you've been able to get access to data that was not easily accessible, such as for customer research, market analysis, product health, etc.

Product manager interviews are heavily behavioral and based on a candidate's past experiences. Generally, interviews will assess the moments when a candidate felt they demonstrated a data-driven mindset. The skills outlined above in the vision section are the primary things you should be looking for in a candidate's story, as supported by their accomplishments. Data-driven decision-making is about being familiar with the idea of metrics, analyzing, and adjusting. Beyond simply knowing what numbers are, it's about being able to make conclusions and tell a story with them, and then leverage that information to make choices and improvements.

Chapter 11: Focus on Customer-Centric Development

11.1. Customer-Centric Development in Product Management

Customer-centric development, another big idea in product management practice today, is very simple in principle: ask what your customers are doing, and why; spend time with your customers, and really understand the product; and always be optimising – so you're building the right products that are fit-for-purpose, and not wasting effort. Demand for a constant pivot ensures that the right products are built – and no others. What percentage of products is not informed by the people using them? How many companies build strategies and products around some flimsy idea at the core? Product management is all about weighing up what the business wants and what the existing customer needs, and what they are likely to need in the future – weighing up those two poles in order to avoid the polemics, and to keep the product vision and strategy aligned with what the customer needs. The closer the product is to what the customer likes, the better. Of course, it's all about understanding those wants and needs.

You may be asked questions in interviews about your thoughts on customer-centric development, what it consists of, and your experience with this. Through a close relationship between customers and product teams, companies are working to create better products that are of substantial value to their customers. It all starts with the study of the customer, through a deep understanding of their daily routines, lifestyle and the logic behind their wants and needs. The values of the customer are defined through the understanding of their sociocultural context. This means that the company will do market research and consider how to modernise structures and create products that not only meet, but exceed, the needs of the customers.

An early and deep focus on the customer in product development improves a product's commercial viability. Immersing customers in the product-development process creates more innovations and builds firm-customer loyalty, which increases a product's success and financial return. This meta-theory puts the customer at the centre of strategic decision-making and shifts the market towards customer-centric products.

11.2. Benefits in Product Management

Recognising and addressing buyer needs allows the product development team to tailor products and services to better suit customers, reducing perceived risk and uncertainty, and better aligning value. Targeting products to customer needs increases the likelihood of a better product-need fit for both niche and mass markets. A strong and compelling value proposition, clearly communicated to the customer, drives engagement, minimises switching costs, and fosters stronger product-customer relationships.

This leads to better product quality, lower resource costs and less competition. But a customer-centric approach can also enhance intrinsic team performance by improving knowledge management and customer data collection. Involving customers in R&D can help increase creativity and ensure that the market is pulling (rather than pushing) new products to completion.

11.3. Assessment of Customer-First Thinking in Interviews

A core ability of product management is the customer-first decision-making. The interviewer will test whether the candidate really takes the company mission seriously, and ultimately customer success. Customers should participate in the process early on to ensure that the product is created with a clear understanding of the feature value.

Interviewers will ask questions to test your belief in customer-driven design, and your ability to leverage customer insights into decision-making. You should be judged on your understanding of customer engagement and your application of customer-driven thinking to concrete product-management situations.

11.4. Key Indicators of a Customer-Centric Approach

Active listening: Candidates who inquire about customer experiences, and care about learning from users.

Empathy: First-order empathy with users, learning what they want or need, and then turning that into product improvements.

Problem Solving: The ability to use customer insights to reinvent the product experience.

Flexibility: Candidates who can pivot based on user feedback, and who are good with change in product strategy.

Candidates who can express how their goals are aligned with customer feedback and company objectives.

11.5. Measuring Success in Customer-Centric Development

For example, interviewers might inquire about how success is being measured, since product managers need to rely on specific metrics to understand whether customer-centric strategies are working.

CSAT: Customer satisfaction score, a PM's best feedback on whether the product is delivering what customers want.

Net Promoter Score (NPS): A measure of customer loyalty and likelihood of recommending the product to others. It is derived from asking the question 'On a scale of 0 to 10, how likely are you to recommend this product to a friend or colleague?'

Customer Retention Rate: Understanding how customer-centric product development leads to long-term customer loyalty.

CES: Customer Effort Score – how much effort is required by users to complete tasks with your product, and how this relates to product satisfaction.

Interview Hint: Prepare to discuss how you've leveraged metrics to iterate on customer-driven development, refine product features, or otherwise address customers' pain points.

11.6. The Role of Data in Customer-Centric Development

Feedback from customers is an essential part of the process, but you can only translate it into product decisions if you know how to leverage data. Interviewers might ask how you use qualitative and quantitative data to guide product development and innovation.

Customer Analytics: Using data on user behavior to identify patterns and opportunities for improvement.

A/B Testing: Testing alternative versions of features or experiences to see how users engage with them.

Customer Segmentation: customer base divided into groups that are alike in important respects so that marketing efforts can be focused on developing tailored experiences to best meet their needs.

Surveys and Polls: Using customer surveys to gather actionable insights and drive product improvements.

Interview Tip: You should be ready to walk through examples of how you analysed data to make customer-centric product decisions, from insight-to-insight, and from feature prioritisation to the final product.

11.7. Leveraging Cross-Functional Teams in Customer-Centric Development

Product managers don't exist in a vacuum. In order to understand and meet customer needs, they need to work well not only within their own product team, but also with other teams, such as marketing, design, engineering and customer success.

Working closely with Design and Engineering: Describe how you work closely with designers to create user experiences that are informed by customer insights and with engineers to make sure features are technically feasible.

Customer Success and Support Teams: These teams are in daily contact with customers and will be the first to hear about user pain points. PMs need to be able to use this knowledge to inform feature development.

Marketing: How PMs work with marketing teams to understand customer segments better, and get feedback from customers through campaigns and interactions.

Interview Tip: Describe how you have worked across teams to bring product strategy in line with customer feedback and market demands, and give examples of how you have collaborated to create better experiences for users.

11.8. Balancing Business Objectives with Customer Needs

A frequent challenge for product managers is to balance customer needs with business objectives (eg, profitability, market growth, technical feasibility). Students should demonstrate how they have managed to do that without alienating either the stakeholders or the customers in the interview.

Prioritisation Frameworks: The Eisenhower Matrix or MoSCoW prioritisation are tools that help PMs figure out which customer needs to address first.

Balancing External Targets and User Delight: How to keep your revenue aims aligned with features that will delight customers.

Managing Trade-Offs: How to say no to customer requests that don't support long-term business goals, and how to communicate those decisions to customers and stakeholders.

Interview Tip: Have an example ready of how you balanced customer needs against business objectives, and how you described those trade-offs to other stakeholders or users.

11.9. Overcoming Challenges in Customer-Centric Development

Not all customer-centric initiatives go as planned. Sometimes you can be bogged down by conflicting feedback, limited resources or difficulties reading customer insights. Interviewers will want to know how you handle these predicaments.

Handling Conflicting Feedback: How to manage contradictory requests from different user segments or stakeholders.

Prioritising Feedback and Product Enhancements: How you decide which features to build, which improvements to make, and how to allocate your time when you're constrained by tight timelines or limited budgets.

Misinterpretation of Customer Needs: Describe a time when you or your team initially misinterpreted customer needs and how you pivoted.

Interview Tip: Practice tales of how you overcame specific challenges in customer-centric product development – how you pivoted the pitch, communicated, and delivered results despite hiccups.

11.10. Translating Customer Feedback into Product Features

And then, after the feedback has been collected, product managers must translate it into product features. This is not as simple as taking a laundry list of requests. To select and prioritise features, you need to map the feedback to your product vision and assess feasibility. This is where tools like the Kano model and value-effort matrices come into play.

Product managers must innovate: take customer feedback and turn it into features. Agile user stories are a technique where teams come together to write down what they believe they heard from the customer, then map feature ideas to part of a product's 'whole' using feature mapping.

Chapter 12: Customer-Centric Development in Product Management

12.1. Introduction to Customer-Centric Development

Customer-centric development in product management has seen significant growth recently. Its basic principles involve understanding what customers are doing and why, while constantly improving products through close customer engagement. Ensuring products align with customer needs, rather than simply business objectives, helps companies create more successful products. A clear product vision and strategy, grounded in customer needs, increases the likelihood of success. The closer the product aligns with customer wants and needs, the more successful it will be.

12.1.1. Definition and Importance

In interviews, you may be asked about your understanding of customer-centric development and how you've practiced it. Customer-centric development starts with understanding the customer's routines, lifestyle, and the logic behind their needs. This process includes market research and structuring strategies to modernize products in ways that exceed customer expectations. Products that meet customers' needs are more commercially viable and contribute to long-term business success. By researching customer needs, companies can create innovative solutions, resulting in loyal customers who generate positive financial returns.

12.1.2. Benefits in Product Management

By identifying and prioritizing customer needs, product teams can tailor their offerings, leading to increased customer satisfaction, reduced uncertainty, and better value alignment. Tailor-made products that meet customer-specific needs are more likely to succeed and maintain strong customer relationships. This customer-centric approach also enhances team performance, reduces resource costs, and fosters competitive advantages through word-of-mouth strategies, better customer retention, and cross-selling opportunities. Moreover, involving customers in the R&D cycle boosts creativity and ensures continuous product improvement.

12.2. Assessment of Customer-First Thinking in Interviews

A key skill in product management is making decisions with a customer-first mentality. In interviews, candidates will be assessed on their ability to empathize with customers and align their decision-making with customer needs. Engaging customers early in the product development process and using their feedback to validate features is a critical approach. Companies can assess candidates' values through targeted questions, evaluating how they integrate customer engagement into decision-making and product strategy.

12.2.1. Key Indicators of a Customer-Centric Approach

1. **Active Listening:** Candidates should demonstrate curiosity about customers' experiences and listen carefully to feedback.
2. **Empathy:** Displaying empathy for customers and understanding their needs is crucial.
3. **Problem Solving:** Candidates should be able to articulate how they apply customer insights to improve product strategies.
4. **Adaptability:** Candidates should showcase their ability to adjust based on user feedback and explain their critical thinking process.
5. **Aligned Goals:** Candidates need to articulate how shared goals align with customer feedback and demonstrate prioritization for maximum impact.

12.2.2. Common Interview Questions

- Can you share a time when you worked closely with a customer and gained insights into their needs?
- How have you seen the results of your work impact customers?
- Describe an instance where you or your team went the extra mile to support a customer. What did you learn from that experience?
- Have you worked on a project where customer feedback led to a significant change in direction? How did you manage that change?

12.3. Translating Customer Feedback into Product Features

Once customer feedback is collected, product managers must translate it into product features. This process involves prioritization, alignment with long-term product vision, and ensuring feasibility. Techniques such as the Kano model, value-effort matrices, and Agile methodologies help manage customer feedback and create a product roadmap. Feature mapping, user stories, and cross-functional collaboration also play essential roles in translating customer insights into actionable development steps.

12.3.1. Importance of Customer Feedback in Product Development

Customer feedback serves as a guiding light for product teams, allowing them to understand what users truly want. By continuously gathering feedback, teams can make strategic, informed decisions that align with customer needs. Both qualitative and quantitative feedback are crucial for understanding the 'why' and 'what' behind customer behaviors, enabling product teams to make better decisions and improve the product-market fit.

12.3.2. Strategies for Processing Feedback

Effective translation of customer feedback into product features involves strategies like the MoSCoW method for prioritization. Ensuring that diverse team members participate in this process allows for a broader understanding of customer needs. Teams should also develop prototypes and MVPs to test feature implementations based on concrete feedback. Iterative development allows teams to adapt and refine features based on real-time customer input.

12.4. Lessons Learned and Best Practices

Engaging customers early in the product development process fosters a deeper understanding of their needs. Continuous customer integration and adaptation based on feedback ensure that products evolve in alignment with the market. Best practices for customer-centric development include:

1. **Early Engagement:** Always engage customers as early as possible.
2. **Continuous Dialogue:** Customer feedback should be part of an ongoing conversation, not a one-time data collection.

3. **Adaptability:** Products must evolve as customer needs change. Flexibility in development ensures continuous product-market fit.

In conclusion, a customer-centric approach to product management involves constant learning, adapting, and innovating based on customer needs. By staying close to the customer and integrating their feedback into the product development cycle, product managers can ensure long-term success and market relevance.

Chapter 13: Dealing with Stakeholders

In the complex world of product management, stakeholder management is a pivotal skill that professionals must master to drive successful product outcomes. Stakeholders, who can range from team members to external clients and investors, have varying expectations and needs. Effectively managing these relationships requires a strategic approach to ensure all parties are aligned with the product's vision and goals. Successful product managers are adept at balancing the interests of diverse stakeholders. This begins with clear and consistent communication, which lays the foundation for strong relationships. Regular updates and dialogue through meetings, emails, or collaborative tools keep stakeholders informed and engaged. Understanding the priorities and pain points of each stakeholder is crucial, which can be achieved through thorough stakeholder analysis and creating personas. Another effective strategy is to establish a common ground or vision for the product, aligning stakeholders' expectations with the product roadmap. Product managers should also be prepared to negotiate and resolve conflicts by maintaining a neutral stance and focusing on data-driven decisions. Stakeholder management is crucial in product development for several reasons. First, it ensures the product development process is streamlined and efficient as each stakeholder knows their role and contribution. It also reduces misunderstandings and discrepancies during development, thus minimizing delays and additional costs. Moreover, effective stakeholder management fosters a collaborative environment where stakeholders feel invested in the product, leading to improved quality and innovation. This collective involvement maximizes the product's market relevance and success, as feedback and insights from varied stakeholders can lead to enhancements that resonate with the target audience. Managing stakeholder relationships is an indispensable component of product management that significantly impacts product success. By employing strategic communication, aligning product visions, and fostering a collaborative environment, product managers can harness stakeholder contributions effectively. Stakeholder management is about forming partnerships that drive the product development process forward.

13.1. Assessment of Stakeholder Management Skills in Interviews

This section introduces our survey, conducted through interviews with professionals in eleven large French organizations, to collect data on the expected stakeholder management activities, the necessary skills, and appropriate methods for assessing them. The semi-structured interviews began with identifying different professional stakeholders (i.e., individuals or groups who can significantly impact the job and who are affected by the job in return), followed by focusing on the abilities necessary to manage them. The respondents, all holding middle management positions in various organizational departments, were asked to identify professional stakeholders and discuss the types of relationships they establish with them. The final stage involved identifying the abilities necessary for employees to manage these relationships effectively. This analysis led to the construction of a grid that includes three major ability areas: relational skills, managerial skills, and sector-related skills (activities, duties of the function, organizational processes, associated competencies, and association with professional stakeholders). The first two areas include both technical and human skills.

13.1.1. Key Indicators of Stakeholder Management Abilities

1. **Political Awareness:** Stakeholders emanate from the multiplicity of interests among parties beyond just shareholders. Political skill represents a manager's ability to perceive, interpret, and act within a political environment, recognizing significant activities and knowing when to engage in specific behaviors.
2. **Integrity:** A key part of managing stakeholder relationships is being honest and trustworthy. Integrity builds trust in the manager's words and actions, essential for forming long-term relationships.
3. **Social Skill:** Managers who understand, interpret, and interact effectively with others are more successful in various dimensions of management. Social skills are crucial for resolving conflicts and building relationships with stakeholders, especially in crisis situations.

13.2. Balancing Conflicting Priorities and Aligning Diverse Teams

In professional settings, team members often have different responsibilities and may be accountable to multiple project leaders and constituents. Identifying and prioritizing organizational goals related to stakeholder interests simplifies decision-making. Teams that align stakeholder goals early on are more likely to deliver successful outcomes. The key to minimizing stakeholder conflicts is reaching a common understanding among all parties about the project's goals and what is needed to complete it. Teams that try to satisfy all stakeholder expectations may face scope creep and a loss of focus on high-value strategic activities. When conflicts arise, it is important to allocate resources based on stakeholder priorities and project goals.

13.2.1. Strategies for Prioritization and Conflict Resolution

In situations where priorities conflict and resources are limited, decision-makers must establish a hierarchy of stakeholders. Primary stakeholders receive priority attention, while secondary and tertiary stakeholders may have their needs addressed as resources allow. Resolving conflicts requires clear communication and managing stakeholder expectations. Engaging key stakeholders early in the process helps prevent surprises and encourages collaborative problem-solving. On the positive side, involving stakeholders in discussions about problem-solving and project goals often leads to innovative solutions and a more cohesive project outcome.

Chapter 14: How Some PMs Are Falling Behind (and How You Can Stay Ahead)

It's a cutthroat industry – the product management business is changing quickly, and product managers (PMs) who aren't keeping up are the ones being left behind. This chapter outlines why some PMs fall behind and what you can do to avoid their mistakes – and stay ahead of the pack – in a tough market. It also offers tips on how to position yourself as a technologically savvy candidate in your next interview, from talking the talk on technology, AI and data.

14.1 Why Certain PMs Struggle to Keep Up

When it comes to why so many PMs fail, it's mostly because of these four things: The 'doers' fail to adapt to the changing nature of the role Companies are no longer hiring PMs who manage the product's life cycle. Rather, the role has evolved to include a broad understanding of technology trends, customer needs, and strategic thinking. Here's what I've come to believe are some of the primary reasons why so many PMs fail:

Obsolete technical skill sets: With the rapid rise of AI, machine learning and general automation for many aspects of an organisation, PMs who have not kept up with technical competence have fallen behind. Understanding of AI tools, data analysis and at least high-level knowledge of a tech stack is a bare minimum in some industries, and in others allows PMs to gradually take on more technical duties (for example, front-end development). A PM who does not keep up with technical changes rapidly falls behind more technically competent candidates.

Failure to Adapt to the Agile Mindset: Agile is less of a methodology and more of a mindset. If you're a PM stuck in rigid, old-school ways of working, it's difficult to keep up with fast-moving companies focused on adaptability, rapid iterations, and customer feedback loops.

Low Data Literacy: Analysing and acting on data is an increasingly central component of the PM function. Those PMs who can't interpret changes in performance metrics, apply AI-powered analytics tools, or predict field trends through machine learning models are left behind while companies become data-native.

Vision (or lack thereof) around AI and automation: PMs need to be operating product teams that are leveraging AI, automation and other emerging technologies in their product strategies. PMs who cannot speak to how AI can improve product experiences or how it can help automate, will not be able to drive value in this market.

14.2 What Interviewers Want to Know

When interviewing for PM roles, however, hiring managers are not looking for someone who is just capable of handling the current workload – they want someone who is future-focused. And this does not just mean someone savvy about the business landscape, but someone ready to harness all that's going on in the tech space, too. Interviewers expect candidates to also have a handle on the trends happening in the sector. Some of the things interviewers consider when evaluating the right person for the job include:

Tech and AI fluency: Increasingly, employers want PMs who know how to work with AI, recognise technical limitations, and spot places where automation can drive speed. Interviewers will test whether you get how emerging tech is changing the landscape, and where it makes sense to include it in product roadmaps.

Ability to Adapt: Have you been asked how you've adapted to change, particularly in the realm of tech advancements? If not, the question is bound to come up. Can you share examples of how you've learned new technologies, or incorporated artificial intelligence (AI) into a product? Interviewers want to know if you are the type of PM who is continually learning and improving, particularly in a tech world.

Data-driven decision-making: Companies expect PMs to be heavily informed by data. Interviewers will ask you how you use data – usually generated by artificial intelligence-powered (AI) tools – to guide product strategy and execution. Prepare to discuss your experience with analytics tools, machine learning applications and datafocused KPIs.

Agile Leadership: Your ability to work in, and lead, agile, tech-forward teams is increasingly a critical skill. Interviewers will ask how you might apply agile principles in your next role, particularly with the application of AI and automation tools. They'll also want to know how well you can lead cross-functional teams in an ever-increasing dynamic environment.

14.3 How to Present Yourself as Forward-Thinking in Interviews

You'll need to be able to convey, in interviews, how you're on top of, or ahead of, it. Here's how to show that you're a proactive problem-solver:

highlight Continuous Learning in AI and Tech: display any certifications or courses (online or traditional) that you have taken in AI, machine learning or other product tech stacks, if applicable. Elaborate how it has influenced your perspective as a product manager, and how you are leveraging tech to build innovative product.

Offer Future-Focused Tech Case Studies: Candidates who can demonstrate true foresight with relevant examples are very likely to differentiate themselves from other applicants, especially through real-world examples from their careers. Discuss ways that you leveraged technological foresight and anticipation to successfully work on projects, for instance, implementing new AI technologies and automation frameworks or data analytics before your product or service area had standardised best practices.

Point out AI-Driven Successes: Mention data-driven or AI-driven projects where you used insights from an AI-powered recommendation engine or machine learning algorithm to make a strategic decision that improved the product. You could have optimised a feature (eg, a search feature that uses AI to surface more personalised and appropriate content for a user) based on customer data analysis, or used predictive analytics insights to improve a product across the board.

Spotlight Tech-Forward Agile Teams: Point out how you've led agile teams with cross-functional teams working with AI and other tech-driven tools. Explain how you've led teams to collaborate, adapt, innovate and iterate. Discuss how you've brought about tech adoption and how you have pivoted when circumstances called for it.

14.4 Key Skills to Highlight in Your Responses

When interviewing for PM roles, you should highlight certain technical skills that are now key to the product management landscape, especially around technology and AI. Here's how to navigate them in your answers:

AI and Technical fluency: Demonstrate proficiency with the tech stacks that underpin product development and that utilise elements of automation and AI. Mention the specific tools or systems you've worked with and how they affect your product decisions (for example, TensorFlow, AWS for machine learning, or any AI-based analytics tools).

Data Literacy and AI-Informed Insights: When it's appropriate, describe your experience with data tools, including those enhanced with AI. Perhaps you've relied on data-informed decisions, machine learning insights or predictive analytics to inform product strategy, enhance user experience or drive cost savings.

Agile Thinking with a Tech Twist: Describe your experience with agile environments and emphasise how you've utilised technology to augment agile processes, focusing on how you can iterate fast, inform business decisions with data and customer input, and leverage AI or automation to increase the efficiency and potency of product production.

How did Emotional Intelligence help you embrace new technologies, or overcome stakeholder concerns about AI?From your standpoint as a leader, what employer are you hoping to address?Have you previously transitioned a team to a new tech stack? Has there been a recent change in management policies that has elicited strong emotions from your team? Have you resolved a customer-facing conflict about integrating a new technology or automating a process? Have you heard concerns that a new tech solution will replace jobs or lead to job insecurity? If yes, how did you navigate this challenge? How did Emotional Intelligence help you overcome stakeholder concerns about implementing new technologies? Did you keep cool-headed when a customer was upset that you were not willing to share your AI expertise with them? Have you successfully built a high-performing team that could survive industry changes?

14.5 Staying Ahead of the Curve: Continuous Improvement

Learning about technology is an ongoing process that the best PMs always take seriously. Here are some practices to ensure that you don't get left behind.

Update your knowledge: Follow tech blogs, webinars and Product Management online communities that specialise on AI and emerging technologies. Keep track of the growing impact of AI, automation and PLG within product management.

Invest in technological capacity: figure out areas you need to grow, whether it's cultivating a deep understanding of AI tools, learning a new programming language, or getting certified in machine learning. These demonstrations will show to interviewers that you're dedicated to remaining competitive in the profession.

Find Tech Mentors: Surround yourself with people who are AI and tech experts. A mentor can help you integrate new tech into product strategies and advise you on how to lead in a tech-driven environment.

EQ is still essential: As organisations focus more on teams and collaboration, emotional intelligence is critical. Build relationships with your technology teams, stakeholders and customers, and be the kind of empathetic, inspirational leader that you capable of being, especially as you lead new technologies.

With these tactics in hand, you'll sidestep the pitfalls that have tripped some PMs up, and come across to your colleagues as a technologist's best friend — a product manager who's ready for anything.

Otherwise, as things change rapidly in tech, you'll eventually become obsolete. So, if you're looking to grow within the product management field, this is the one thing you can do to keep ahead. Continuous improvement and learning is the best way to stay on top of everything that's happening in this space and to make sure that you're the product manager who brings the best solutions to the table from interview to interview.

Chapter 15: The Role of Communication and Cross-Functional Collaboration

While product management can be a very individualistic job, it's not an especially good product manager that succeeds alone. This is what makes interview questions about collaboration so important: increasingly, companies are going to want to know about your ability to communicate across teams and to listen to people who do not look, think, know or operate as you do. It takes a degree of comfort with shifting power dynamics, with contradictory mandates, and with using uneven knowledge to lead to a successful product — and that's what the interview questions are trying to assess. In this chapter, I'll explain how to answer collaboration interview questions, how to prepare solid collaboration examples (and what those will look like), and what your interviewers are actually looking for when they probe you on your ability to lead in the increasingly hybrid team environments.

15.1 Common Interview Questions on Communication and Collaboration

Part of the job description of product managers is countless communication with many internal teams, and so the interviewers want to hear how you typically manage relationships with others. A few common questions that interviewers would ask candidates on the aspects of communication and cross-functional collaboration can be seen below.

'Have you ever had to work alongside engineers or graphic designers to get a product out the door to users?'

That's the question you'll need to answer, by applying your skills at translating requirements, balancing competing concerns and keeping everyone on the same page.

"How do you handle conflicts or misalignment between team members from different functions?"
Your answer to this question reveals how you resolve tensions and keep the team steered in the right direction in the face of difference.

'Tell me about a time when you had to balance different stakeholders with conflicting interests.'

It's a way of exploring your stakeholder management skills – balancing needs among customers, executive leadership and cross-functional teams.

Like: 'In this project, how do you stay abreast of everything and keep your teams on the same page?'

In this context, interviewers are interested in how you maintain transparent communication or collaboration with others – to make sure that everyone is on the same page.

15.2 How to Present Examples of Working with Engineers, Designers, and Marketing Teams

In interviews, you must demonstrate cross-functional collaboration stories, and this is how you do it. Cross-Functional Collaboration This candidate personifies effective collaboration across two different teams:

Engineers:
PMs can be the intermediary between engineering teams and the rest of the organisation Below you will paraphrased instruction that describes a task, paired with an input that provides further context. Write a response that appropriately completes the request: Paraphrase the input into human-sounding text while retaining citations and quotes. Below is an instruction that describes a task, paired with an input that provides further context. Write a response that appropriately completes the request: If you work with engineers as a PM, make sure to highlight your potential to process technical constraints, communicate business goals and ongoing priorities, and order features based on value to customers and the company. For example:

'Meanwhile I worked with the engineering team in order to make sure we didn't get to the point where technical debt was exceeding the feature roadmap; via coordinated discussions with stakeholders and the development team, features continued to be re-ordered without sacrificing product integrity.'

Designers:
For designers, talk about how you helped create user-centred products, such as how you translated customer feedback into design changes or how you all worked together to improve the look and feel of a product. For example:

I worked with the design team to re-engineer the UX, and we interpreted our user research to inform our design choices. I also conducted regular design reviews and balanced creative intentions with business outcomes.

Marketing Teams:
Product managers are involved with marketing to coordinate launch dates, collaborate on positioning and messaging, as well as much more. When discussing your time in marketing, highlight how you worked with marketing delivery teams to maximise product-market fit, and help your product launch successfully. For example:

'I worked closely with the marketing team during our product launch phase to develop a go-to-market strategy. I made sure our messaging for the product tied to the new features and benefits and that our marketing campaigns addressed user pain points.

Executive Teams:
More and more all Product Management functions get to interface with high stake players such as Executive Team members. Organisations are flatter than ever and now even junior PMs are finding they need to work with high ranking individuals.

15.3 Leading and Contributing in Hybrid Teams: What Interviewers Look For

Many interviews these days are for positions that will require you to work for a hybrid team: with members located across multiple locations or multiple time zones. Startup teams often fall into this category. Interviewers want to know what you're like to work with in such a team. Here is what they look for:

Effective Communication:

PMs need to keep hybrid teams on the same page when they're not physically together.Talk about how you use digital tools (Slack, Zoom, Asana) to enable collaboration and communication across remote or distributed teams.

Check Zoom calls were scheduled twice a week. To keep track of tasks, I used Trello: a board that is visible by our entire hybrid team and managed by a platform. That way, if we can't reach all teammates, even from different countries or cities, remote workers are not left out.

Cultural and Time Zone Awareness:
When leading hybrid teams, it is important to be sensitive to time-zone differences and cultural distinctions and interviewers will want to see evidence that you can coordinate effectively and value these differences in working hours and styles.

'Scheduling meetings for different time zones for working with teams across the globe, adapting to a global culture and making sure our remote employees also felt their participation mattered.'

Collaboration in a Hybrid Setup:
You need to demonstrate to your interviewers your ability to direct in-person and remote staff members so our hybrid teams get the best results from blended settings. Be sure they know you create a culture of team accountability and that you maintain full visibility on all channels of communication.

'In that hybrid world, I was really focused on community-building and transparency,' he explains, 'by putting up shared documents and dashboards where everyone could see things whether they were here or there.'

Adaptability and Flexibility:

Examples of hybrid teams may see mixed approaches to leadership, because project managers and team leaders may be using different approaches for the non-co-located versus co-located members of the team. Interviewers will want to get a sense of how well you adapt to the needs of your team members – whether they work in-office or remote – and whether you are able to flexibly change your leadership style to match these different types of environments.

The upside was that, when we went back to a somewhat hybrid model, I learned to adapt. For example, I conducted more and more asynchronous meetings, so that the remote member could participate on her own schedule, and I encouraged using Miro and other collaborative tools for brainstorms.

15.4 Mastering Communication and Collaboration in Interviews

On the other hand, to claim the upper hand in interviewing regarding one's communication and interpersonal effectiveness, the key is to keep these in mind:

Get specific: share examples of how you've worked already with different teams Standard examples of projects work well, since these show the depth of your experience. Mention cross-functional teams and collaboration with engineers, designers and marketers.

Highlight your Leadership of Hybrid Teams: Discuss your experience leading remote teams or hybrid work environments, especially in this post-pandemic environment where remote flexibility has become the norm.

Highlight Communication Tools/Methods – call out particular tools, how you used them, what successes you had, eg: weekly standups, callouts, use of Slack for QTMs, task tracking with Jira, etc.

 Demonstrate Versatility: Show your readiness to accommodate changing team dynamics and external factors (eg, working with a geographically distributed team, working with distinct time zones, or working asynchronously).

Chapter 16: Ensuring Long-Term Product Success

As markets become fiercer, users become harder to please, and slimmer become the profit margins, product managers are constantly being challenged to ensure their products never just survive but thrive. The question has become not just about launching great products, but how do we maintain their engagement, their ongoing and sustained customer loyalty, and how do we do so without turning ourselves into the product update equivalent of Captain Kirk's transporter officer, reasoning: 'You want more? You can handle more. You're ready for more. So, uh, I'm just going to beam a little more over here, just to be safe.' Product managers wonder: 'So I hope you don't mind if I do jump in here.' The product manager might ask: 'How do I avoid the runaway treadmill of product features, losing my users? How do I make my product sticky? How can I create the most sticky products possible – the most adaptive to the ever-changing needs of the market but without duplicating feature bloat?

These, however, are especially crucial challenges today, at a time when users expect more and more seamless and personalised experiences, and also when businesses feel increasing pressures to innovate in a timely and effective fashion while keeping costs under control. Top product managers drive the effort by wielding the sword of analytics, the shield of user feedback, and the spear of agile methodologies to build products that continuously get better, stickier, and more competitive. Better is not synonymous with more stuff. More sticky isn't necessarily more addictive. Real value does not have to be over-the-top, undifferentiated, or incongruent to the user's life.

What employers want in a product manager today is someone who is deft at handling these complications, someone who appreciates the tension between innovation and ease, who can bring together multiple teams to iterate quickly and build products that are not only used, but re-used.

One hallmark of a great product manager is the ability to react to shifting market dynamics, to pivot without sacrificing quality, and to maintain strong user retention metrics. In this chapter, we explore the strategies and mindsets that product management teams are adopting to achieve these goals and share a set of tools to help you prepare for a variety of potential interview questions on these topics; from the psychology of product stickiness, to user retention fundamentals to product adaptation in the face of fast-moving markets, this chapter aims to illustrate what it means to be a great product manager.

Even in interviews, you need to speak more in terms of the why than the how: What did you expect to be the issues and how did you actually deal with them in the real world? Employers are searching for PMs who can talk about the why, about their understanding of what it means to lead a product's life cycle – how they've considered user needs, used company resources, and reacted to market forces.

16.1 Understanding Product Stickiness

Product stickiness is about creating engaging experiences that keep a user on a product. The most sticky products start to define a user's life – they become part of a user's workflow, a behaviour, or even an addiction. When interviewing product-management candidates, you should expect them to describe how they designed a product to create a habit, or how they designed a product to get users to delve deeply.

Key strategies for enhancing stickiness include:
Habit-forming features– Triggers and rewards embedded in the product to encourage repeat use (for example, through notifications, personalised content, or gamification).

Personalisation: Tailoring the experience of the product to the individual user, based on the user's own preferences and behaviour, thereby improving user satisfaction and the sense of affinity or attachment to the product.

Seamless onboarding: Ensuring that onboarding is familiar and pleasant and that our users are getting the most value out of the product from day one, setting us up to keep them on the hook.

Example Interview Question:
"How have you incorporated features that promote product stickiness in the past?"
Example Answer:
'Previously, I worked on a mobile fitness app that aimed to increase engagement with users and create daily habits around logging exercise. We designed a gamification feature based on badges to reward users for logging their workouts daily and weekly, and used machine learning to personalise workout recommendations based on their activity patterns. Furthermore, push notifications were used to remind users about progress and

upcoming challenges, leading to a 30 per cent increase in daily active users within three months. The app evolved into a habit.'

Example Interview Question:
'Name some products you were involved in that turned out to be "drug-like", that is, products so irresistible that some users couldn't help but use them to excess.'

Example Answer:
In a language-learning app I used to lead, we had a daily streak feature, rewarded when users studied with us every day; we sent push notifications to keep the streak alive; and personalised content recommendations according to their skill level. These are all highly effective ways to get users to come back more regularly. This boosted our DAU/MAU ratio from 10 to 20 per cent in six months.

16.2 Mastering User Retention

User retention is one of the most critical metrics for evaluating the long-term success of a product. Retention represents the percentage of users returning to your product over time. In other words, it refers to keeping the users you already have happy, and learning how to keep them from churning over time. Since retention is really important to you as a product manager, your interviewer will want to hear about your views and techniques for how to keep your users engaged.

Some key tactics to improve user retention include:
Iterative improvements: constantly improving the product (by releasing new versions, for example) to reduce pain points and bring features in line with the changing needs of users.

Customer feedback loops: How you consistently gather feedback from users, reviewers, customers and subscribers, looking for pain points and opportunities to improve. Detail what feedback you have, from which channels, and how you have acted upon that feedback.

Retention-oriented metrics monitoring: Monitoring DAU/MAU (Daily Active Users/Monthly Active Users), churn rate and user engagement scores to detect signs of attrition and act accordingly.

Example Interview Question:
"What steps would you take to improve retention for a product with high churn?"

Example Answer:
When it comes to churn, I've found that the best approach is to do a data deep-dive to determine at which stage in the user lifecycle churn is occurring. In a previous project for a subscription-based video streaming service, I observed that, shortly after the availability of the user's free trial, there was a significant drop-off. We asked users in a survey what their pain points were, and they reported that they were not fully aware of the service's unique features. We redesigned the onboarding experience, which now highlighted these features, and we included tutorials for them. We also created a 'win-back' campaign with personalised content recommendations for users who were showing signs of disengagement. The changes resulted in a 15 per cent decrease in churn over the course of three months.

Example Interview Question:
"How do you measure and improve user retention for a product you manage?"

Example Answer:

I start by defining a few key retention metrics (DAU/MAU, churn rate). For instance, when running a SaaS product at one of my previous jobs, we found that the DAU/MAU ratio of our users was lower than expected. We addressed this by implementing an automated feature that would send users regular reports on how their KPI was positively affected by our product. Another initiative was user onboarding webinars to further strengthen the product training. By constantly tracking churn and conducting follow-ups with exiting users, we came up with improvements that resulted in an increase in retention of 12 per cent.

16.3 Product Adaptation and Growth

As markets and user needs change, product managers need to ensure that their products can adapt. This can be achieved by evolving a product over time – that is, responding to changes in market conditions, technology, and user expectations by adjusting the product. In interviews, you will need to show how you have successfully led product evolution and ensured sustained growth.

Key strategies for product adaptation include:
Continuous user research: learning about your users and their needs through user interviews, usability testing, and analytics. This allows you to be proactive instead of reactive.

Iterative development: Product roadmaps that are built into flex via pivots or in response to market feedback, new entrants, or changes in user behaviour.

Scalability: How big can this get? How does it support growth of the user base from 500 to 500,000 users (or a billion!) if appropriate? This applies to potential expansion of technical capacity as new features are added to the product.

Example Interview Question:
'Could you tell us about a time when you had to adapt a product to a significant market change?'

Example Answer:
While working on a mobile ecommerce app, a company I used to work for observed that an increasing number of customers were preferring to transact on social media instead of in the app. So, we pivoted the company's product roadmap to allow clients to buy products from Instagram and Facebook posts directly. In doing so, not only did customer engagement rise, but also we opened up a new revenue stream via social commerce, and the company saw a rise in transactions by 25 per cent within the first six months of the integration.

Example Interview Question:
"How do you ensure a product is scalable for long-term growth?"
Example Answer:
"We need to understand user metrics, where the load will be and how much we plan to scale. Without a plan it is often difficult to gauge our efforts. We should try to build the architecture in such a way that the system can possible handle rising traffic with microservices, meaning each part of the system could scale individually and we could add more regions to accommodate us moving into international markets. I would also work with the data team to make sure that our analytics systems would be able to handle larger datasets as we grow. We want to be able to gauge our user actions, gauge our systems, and gauge what is most valuable or meaningful. Not all features are created equally, sometimes we may also need to kill features to allow ourselves to focus our efforts."

Usability and User-Centric Design
Usability is hugely important to product success. It's the degree to which a product can be used by specified users to achieve

specified goals with effectiveness, efficiency, and satisfaction in a specified context of use. A product can have all the best features in the world, but if the user experience is subpar and difficult to use, they'll likely quit and go to a competitor. Product managers should think through usability by applying user-centric design principles, testing and iterating on different designs, and making sure users have the best experience with a product. In interviews, talk about how you can perform usability testing, treat user behaviour as data, and think through design as a problem-solving process. By highlighting your ability to build products that are not only functional but also usable, you're more likely to score points with your interviewer.

Key Elements of Usability in Product Management:

User-Centric Design: User-centred design is the process of understanding users' needs, motivations and behaviors in order to create products that actually alleviate their pain, speed up their workflow, and make user engagement and satisfaction as high as possible. By utilizing methods such as empathy mapping, user journey mapping and user personas, product managers can work closely with UX/UI designers so that everything from the buttons to the user path that leads someone to that button is intuitive, instinctual, and takes the user to where they want to go. When the product is user-centred, successful products emerge and users engage and behave more frequently with higher satisfaction because it makes their tasks easier and more enjoyable.

Usability Testing: Usability testing is the process of evaluating a product by testing it with actual users. Product managers should test their products at different stages of development to catch any bugs or issues that need to be fixed, as well as to gather ideas for making it even easier to use. Some ways to test usability include A/B testing, heuristic evaluation, and moderated or unmoderated user testing sessions. Testing regularly can help refine the product before it is launched to make it as easy to use as possible.

Iterative Design and Feedback Loops: Iterative design is the process of making many small changes to a product over time, based on user feedback. Unlike the design for a major overhaul of a product, effective product managers work on small changes to improve how users can use their products. Survey, interview and in-app behaviour data collected can help team members identify which features need to be tweaked and how the product can be made more intuitive. A product that is iteratively designed can be on target with what users want over time.

Simplicity/Clarity: Often, usability work is about making complicated things easy. Interfaces should not be littered with choices and widgets that will only distract users from the goal that brought them there. Buttons and links should be wired up in a way that makes sense, rather than allowing users to fall into the wrong part of the system. If a complicated task is required, break it up into small steps, or provide tooltips and guides that will lead users through the process in a logical manner.

Accessibility: A product should be usable for as many people as possible. This includes making sure the product is accessible for people with hearing loss, visual, motor and cognitive impairments, for example, through screen readers, keyboard navigation, colour contrast and other means (eg, WCAG). Product managers should have a good understanding of accessibility standards and work with their design and development teams to make the system as accessible as possible.

Example Interview Question:
"Tell me about a time you revamped something to make a product easier to use. What did you do, and how did it change user engagement?"

Example Answer:

"In a previous role, I worked on a project for a project management tool that received feedback from users that task creation was too confusing and time-consuming. After conducting user interviews and usability tests, we found that users were getting lost in the multiple steps required to input data into a task. 'After this feedback, we redesigned the task creation process into a single, streamlined pop-up window with distinct labels for each section. We also wrote user-friendly tooltips to guide users along the way. We even added a feature that allowed users to duplicate task templates, thus improving their workflow. 'Using the new task creation process, these changes led to a 30 per cent decrease in task creation time and a 20 per cent increase in daily active users in two months."

Example Interview Question: "How do you make sure that a feature is actually usable or not cluttering the user interface?"

Example Answer: "Before adding a new feature, I start from its fundamental purpose and how it benefits the user. He worked closely with the design team to apply the feature to the existing workflow, drawing up wireframes and prototypes that the team tested with a small set of users. In one of his projects, a finance app, he wanted to introduce a budgeting tool, which would auto-categorise expenses, and hence reduce users' need for manual input. Over a few rounds of feedback, the feature was refined further, simplifying the interface with preset categories and a drag-and-drop feature so that users could easily sort out their expenses. Post-launch, he monitored the feature's usage and continued to refine it over time, based on user data. By applying this principle, he ensured that the new feature didn't add unnecessary clutter to the app."

Product managers can optimise for usability design, to make sure products work really well, including how users can intuitively navigate the tool so it solves their real problems. By touching on user-centric design, the iterative process, and accessibility, this section trains candidates to talk about their strategy for improving product usability in interviews.

16.4 Understanding Business Models in Product Management

The definition of the right business model is a critical step in a product achieving long-term success. A product's business model defines how it will make money, acquire and retain customers, and be self-sustaining over time. Product managers need to be skilled at analyzing and selecting the right business model for the product and the market. The business model needs to be aligned with the objectives of the company, and it also needs to be feasible in terms of meeting user needs. Candidates are often asked during interviews to describe how they contributed to defining or refining a business model for a product, demonstrating how they think strategically about the business.

Key business models include:

- **Subscription-Based:** Users pay a fee at regular intervals (e.g., monthly, quarterly, annually) to access a product or service. A common model for software-as-a-service (SaaS) products, subscription models target user retention over the long term. Successful product managers in subscription businesses must prioritize customer engagement, satisfaction, and minimizing churn on an ongoing basis.
- **Freemium:** The basic features of the product are free, and users can pay for optional features or enhancements. This model aims to gain a large customer base through a free version and convert a percentage of those users to paying customers. Product managers must balance the amount of value provided for free against the enticement of additional premium features to maximize conversion rates.
- **Pay-Per-Use:** This is based on the actual use by the user. A typical example is cloud computing services and pay-per-click

advertising that you see on Google. The job of product managers is to make sure the pricing is simple and easy to understand so that it becomes easy for users to know how to use the product and it encourages them to use it more.

- **Marketplace:** This is a model where a platform connects buyers and sellers and has the opportunity to make money through commissions, transaction fees, or listing fees. Product managers are tasked with building a scalable platform that satisfies the needs of both sides of the marketplace. This includes building trust and reliability for users to transact with each other.
- **Advertising-Supported:** The product is free for the user (e.g., Facebook, Google Search, most mobile apps), and the revenue is generated through advertisements. Product managers here are focused on maximizing the product experience while inserting ads as unobtrusively as possible, ensuring these ads don't diminish the value that the user derives from the product.
- **E-commerce/Retail:** Products are sold directly to consumers, whether physical or digital. Product managers who work with e-commerce models must understand the full customer journey, from getting them into the funnel to checkout, and then driving loyalty with follow-ups, retargeting, and promotions.
- **Hybrid Models:** Today, most products include a mix of models. A SaaS product could have a freemium model with additional pay-per-use services, or an e-commerce store could include subscription services for regular deliveries of products. Product managers are often tasked with understanding where and how to blend the models to optimize revenue and meet customer needs.

Example Interview Question:
"Give me an example of a time when you designed or modified a business model for a product you managed."

Example Answer:
"My previous company was an online learning platform that worked on a pay-per-course model. Though users were paying for the individual courses, we found that users weren't sticking around long term. We were able to leverage our user survey results and engagement metrics to realize that switching to a subscription model where users could have access to all courses for a monthly fee would encourage more frequent use and provide more

predictable revenue. We also implemented a freemium tier that gave users access to a few lessons for free, and this helped us improve our conversion rates to the subscription plan. Overall, by making these changes, we boosted our user retention by 40 percent and improved our monthly revenue by 25 percent."

Example Interview Question:
"Let's say you have a product that you want to bring to market. How should you determine what kind of business model would be appropriate?"

Example Answer:
"When deciding the best business model for a particular product, the first thing I do is think about the target market, my competitors, the value proposition of the product, and how users will engage with the product and the price they will be willing to pay. Often, the answer depends on how frequently users will be accessing the product. If the product provides a daily need, having a subscription model might work best. If it's a very niche product, then a pay-per-use model might be a better fit. I also consider how the different models will affect scaling and user acquisition. Once I have a good sense of the business model, I build some experiments to validate my assumptions. For example, if I believe that the product should be a freemium or tiered pricing model, I might run a test to see if users respond well to that. Once I have a sense of the product's business model, I can scale it up."

Reasoning:
The focus on business models here reveals a keen understanding of business and the broader strategic context that determines why firms exist and what they do. Analyzing, adapting, and innovating around business models can be the key to generating sustainable growth. Good candidates will be able to show how they have selected business models, or refined them, to respond to market needs and increase profitability.

Chapter 17: Navigating the Modern PM Landscape

Besides the traditional issues, the 21st-century product manager has to grapple with integrating advanced technologies such as artificial intelligence, large language models and conversational agents into their product's development. The rise of AI-based tools is starting to shift the nature of the company itself. Decisions can be accelerated, routine tasks automated and customer experiences improved with AI-based intelligent systems. Open-source platforms are the new innovation game-changers, providing flexible, cost-effective solutions that help teams scale rapidly and stay ahead.

You will need to clearly articulate it in the interviews you have: you used predictive analytics to enhance product roadmaps leveraging AI; you improved user interaction employing conversational agents; you built products faster and better leveraging open-source frameworks, etc. Moreover, you should be prepared to discuss how these technologies are transforming cross-functional collaboration, and how you stay ahead of the curve continuously upskilling in emerging technologies. Companies are looking for PMs who are able to not only absorb this disruption, but proactively lead it. Demonstrating that you can do this will also demonstrate that you are ready to perform in this fast-paced, technology-driven environment.

17.1 Interview Questions Related to Adapting to Shorter Product Cycles and Rapid Pivots

The market changes fast, so PMs need to be able to pivot and react to new issues. Here are some common interview questions that can evaluate your propensity for handling rapid product iteration and pivots:

'Tell me about a situation where you had to change the strategy for a product. What happened?'

Here, a question regarding your decision-making and agility gauges how sensitive and flexible you are to business or customer needs. Interviewers want to know that you are able to make decisions based on data and communicate those decisions to the team in a timely manner.

Example Response:
'Once we were in the middle of a feature, sometimes we'd get a new customer insight that showed a change in the market demand, and so I would work with that team to reorder the priorities, and cut the non-essential features, and try to get the key value out more quickly, so that we could be competitive with the emerging customer need.

"How do you manage product development when timelines are shortened?"
The idea behind this question is, how do you handle stress, prioritise, and not let quality become a casualty of speed?

Example Response:
'It's all about brutal prioritization and clear and concise communication. We work with transversal teams to define what is the MVP (Minimum Viable Product) – what's absolutely the minimum for launch without compromising the essential features?

And then the developers' job is to cut down the design to make the deadline.'

"Tell me about a product that failed and how you handled it."
This question tests your capacity to deal with failure and bounce back, an important attribute in organisations where experimentation is central.

Example Response:
'We launched a feature that under-delivered. Adoption was below forecasts. I studied feedback and metrics, and the team then rapidly pivoted with a more intuitive solution as part of the next build. The first roll-out was below expectations, leading to lower customer trust. However, the fast pivot and customer-friendly solution allowed us to rapidly regain trust and ultimately saw higher customer engagement.'

17.2 How Post-Pandemic Changes Are Influencing Product Management Interviews

The way companies operate has been forever altered by the COVID-19 pandemic, and because of this, the questions asked in PM interviews have also changed. Here are the three most notable post-pandemic changes to interview questions:

Remote and Hybrid Work Dynamics:
If you interview for work now that is likely to be carried out at a distance – whether fully remote or partially so – you'll likely be asked about your experience with geographically distributed teams, your ability to manage these teams, and your capacity to keep projects moving despite the challenges of distributed work.

Common Question:

"How have you managed teams or product development in a remote or hybrid environment?"
Example Response:
'We went full remote for the pandemic, and I instituted clear communications (daily standups, asychronous project update in Jira) to make sure everyone knew what was happening and felt like part of the team. I also went out of my way to maintain a strong culture (even through check-ins and virtual team-building activities).

Accelerated Digital Transformation:
The pandemic compelled many industries to digitally transform at increased speed, asking PMs to be more sophisticated digitally, to be able to quickly integrate new technologies and deliver digital solutions.

Common Question:
How did you evolve your product strategy as the digital world shifted during the pandemic?

Example Response:
The pandemic accelerated our digital push. I steered us towards being more digital-first, by using AI for customer service, and figuring out how to extend our mobile app so people could do more through their phone. I explored how we could capture different market opportunities.

Customer-Centric Development in Uncertain Times:
In an uncertain environment, interviewers want to know that you'll stay customer-centric even in volatile market conditions. They'll ask you how you managed product strategy during an economic downturn or uncertain times.

Common Question:

"How do you ensure the product remains customer-centric in a rapidly changing environment?"

Example Response:

'We went to the customer in the pandemic literally every day, and watched the way they were purchasing and using our product change in a fairly drastic way, and gave a lot more feedback in real time ... To give you a sense for what that looks like in a business environment, we would actually iterate every day for one particular customer, listening to their needs, adjusting our product strategy or the product roadmap to suit those customer needs, and then iterating again the next day. So, we were always very involved in keeping the strategy on track and not losing sight of long-term strategic thinking.'

Demand for Rapid Innovation and Deployment

Common Question: "How did the COVID-19 pandemic influence the pace of release of digital products?"

Example Response: "The pandemic forced us to innovate faster than ever before. As a Product Manager, we had to dramatically improve our development timelines and identify what was really important. For instance, I started using agile methodologies to get a minimum viable product (MVP) delivered in weeks rather than months—by releasing iteratively—then gathered feedback from users and went back into the development cycle. This way, we could get valuable insights and make changes where it really mattered—real-world usage."

Shift to Digital-First Business Models

Example Question: "How did the pandemic drive your business model to digital-first, and how did you adapt your product strategy to match?"

Example Response: "The pandemic compelled many businesses to go digital-first. I pivoted our product roadmap to focus more on e-commerce and subscription-based offerings. For example, we shifted from a one-time purchase model to a subscription, which resulted in a 30% increase in customer lifetime value over the first six months. This also allowed us to periodically add new features, keeping users engaged."

Data-Driven Product Development

Example Question: "How did the pandemic influence your approach to data-driven product management?"

Example Response: "When everything went digital, we suddenly had access to vast amounts of real-time data. I applied advanced analytical tools to track user behavior and engagement in real-time. For instance, by analyzing conversion funnel data, we identified a feature that was causing user drop-offs. After making necessary adjustments based on the data, we saw a 15% increase in feature adoption."

Focus on Scalability and Digital Infrastructure

Example Question: "As digital needs rose with the pandemic, how did you organize scaling to support your product?"

Example Response: "The pandemic led to a huge spike in user traffic, so we had to ensure our products could scale efficiently. I worked with my DevOps team to transition to a microservices architecture and migrated to cloud infrastructure, which allowed us to handle a 50% increase in user activity without downtime. We also implemented automated monitoring systems to address performance issues in real-time."

Customer-Centric Digital Experiences

Example Question: "What impact have digital-first customer interactions had on your team's UX design process?"

Example Response: "Almost all customer contact became digital, making user experience a top priority. I improved user journeys by analyzing user behavior daily to identify pain points. For instance, I redesigned the onboarding flow based on customer feedback, which led to a 20% increase in user retention within just a few weeks."

17.3 Strategies to Highlight in Interviews for Staying Relevant in a Shifting Job Market

Especially with the increasingly volatile job market, companies look for PMs that are agile, future-thinking, and can pivot with the changing tides of their industry. Important points to convey in an interview include:

Agility and Flexibility:
Demonstrate flexibility to deal with change and make decisions quickly, in high-pressure situations Highlight examples of times you worked within a fast-paced setting, and explain how you navigated pivots or shifts in strategy.

Example:
I've spent my career in industries where product launches would be brought forward or delayed as customer needs or the market changed. Through closely working with cross-functional teams and applying agile frameworks, I've managed to keep the organisation and team focused and deliver when required.

Data-Driven Decision-Making:
In a market that's inherently uncertain, PMs need to move fast with data, so stress any experience you have with data-analytics software, A/B testing and iteration, and how you can use data insights live, as they become available.

Example:
I keep using data to inform product decisions. For example, at the beginning of the pandemic, we were running A/B tests on usage of features. So we were seeing trends in terms of how certain features were being used, and it helped us re-align our roadmap to really focus on resources on features that offered more value to our customers.

Continuous Learning and Upskilling:
In the fast-paced business environment today, it is important to demonstrate that you are continually updating your skills and keeping abreast of the current state of affairs. List any certifications, courses or technologies you've learnt recently, to prove you are keeping up with the industry.

Example:
To stay ahead in the post-Covid work world, I have pursued certifications in agile product management and courses on AI and machine learning to better understand how emerging technologies could be leveraged for our products.

Cross-Functional Collaboration:
In an era of remote and hybrid work, there's an even greater emphasis on soft skills such as the ability to collaborate with colleagues who don't all sit in the same office or even the same time zone. Focus on your communication skills, and on your penchant for cross-functional collaboration when possible, and particularly when those teams are distributed.

Example:
'With a cross-functional team spread over three time zones throughout the pandemic, I established communications channels as well as shared collaborative workspaces using platforms such as Miro and Slack, which helped us stay in sync while enabling us all to operate effectively despite the challenges.'

Resilience and Innovation in Uncertain Times:
Companies want PMs who can navigate uncertainty and still bring
about innovation. Demonstrate that you're adaptable and willing to
find innovative solutions, even when the environment requires it.

Example:
'The very beginning of the pandemic was a situation of great
market uncertainty: There, I worked with the team to find
opportunities in adjacent markets and develop a product feature
that solved an emerging customer need and opened a new
revenue stream for us.

Chapter 18: Climbing the Leadership Ladder in Product Management

Many product managers, once they gain experience and mastery in product management, want to attain higher leadership roles – whether that's as a manager of larger product teams, or as an executive such as the Chief Product Officer (CPO). The path to higher leadership in the product organisation demands not only technical product-related skills, but also a strategic mindset, good communication and the ability to motivate and lead others. This chapter maps out the route to senior leadership roles and provides some tips on how you might go about the climb to the top.

18.1 Introduction: The Path to Leadership

This section is dedicated to the journey from product manager to senior leadership, highlighting the various milestones a PM must pass along the way to prepare for their next move up the ladder. Specifically, this section provides a roadmap for PMs on how their role changes as they move up the ladder, going from managing features to managing entire product lines and setting company strategy. As PMs rise through the ranks, they are expected to evolve from being hands-on, tactical feature managers to tactical strategists that manage projects, teams and sometimes entire portfolios. In this evolution, PMs are expected to think bigger and require more business acumen to understand the company's product portfolio, the competitive landscape, customer needs and how to make big strategic bets.

18.2 Defining Leadership Roles in Product Management

The day-to-day work of product management varies depending on the role and level of seniority. Here's a breakdown of common leadership roles, and what each typically does:

Junior Product Manager: an entry-level PM who assists senior colleagues on data analysis, user research or project coordination. They work on small projects and gain experience in the basics of product management. The junior position is often a support role to the execution of product plans, which helps them build a platform to advance into more technical positions.

Associate Product Manager (APM): A step above junior PMs, one who runs 'discrete projects, modules, or components of a product'. An APM helps to 'implement the features, gather user feedback, and support strategic initiatives'. Many companies run formal APM programmes to train their future product leaders to own 'a small piece of a product … and to move in-between the technical, design and business domains.

Product Designer: Works closely with PMs to design intuitive user interfaces and experiences. You might not consider this a PM role (yet) but product designers are integral to the product development effort to make products look and feel seamless and easy to use. Their understanding of user experience will inform how the product is built and iterated upon, so it's a great collaboration between the two roles.

Product Manager (PM): The product team can and should be many things: the engine of new product development, an advocate for outside scrutiny into the business, a fount of market insights, and more. The PM is the person who figures out what the team should be striving to do and stays in touch with the external

121

world. This means that PMs have to be good at planning out features, doing market research, and coordinating across the whole organisation. Essentially, they act as the glue holding projects together, which means they have to be good at juggling different priorities and expectations.

Senior Product Manager (Sr. PM): Manages multiple projects or entire product lines. Strategic work includes defining long-term goals, setting the product vision, and mentoring junior PMs. Senior PMs are very important in aligning teams across the organisation and ensuring that products succeed. They lead cross-functional teams to solve complex problems, which involves making trade-offs between short-term and longer-term product strategy.

Product Lead: Leads several product teams or a particular element of a larger product, ensuring consistency and cohesion across teams. As the contact point between senior management and PMs, Product Leads must balance high-level strategy with team-specific execution. Product Leads make sure that various product activities are well-integrated; they also typically spearhead company-wide efforts to standardise processes across teams.

Group Product Manager (GPM): Manages a group of PMs and/or works across multiple projects. GPMs are focused on coordination across teams and developing consistent product strategies for multiple products. This is an important role for cross-functional work that spans multiple product lines and GPMs must excel at stakeholder management as they often work with executive stakeholders to make sure product strategies are aligned with company strategy.

Director of Product Management: Overall responsibility for product portfolios, including the management of large teams, and defining the strategy for the product. Directors will be involved in long-term planning and allocation of resources, ensuring that product goals are in line with the business objectives. Directors of PM are obliged to see the big picture, and they lead strategic initiatives that are designed to expand products and services across the organisation.

VP of Product: Define the product org's strategy, set direction for directors and senior PMs, and lead companywide effortsVice presidents (VPs) of product are responsible for defining the strategic direction of the product organisation, setting the direction for directors and senior PMs, and leading companywide efforts. VPs spend the majority of their time on companywide strategic efforts, competitive positioning, and leading business growth. They also represent the product division in executive meetings, ensuring that product-wide goals are aligned to company strategy.

Chief Product Officer (CPO): The highest product level in the organisation. CPOs own the company-level product vision and strategy, as well as are responsible for product innovation and driving the company's vision forward at the C-suite level. CPOs focus on the growth of the company, including sales and profitability growth, as well as on product innovation and growth. CPOs also oversee all product-related activities and are accountable for the product PnL, ensuring they are one of the most important roles in the company.

18.3 Key Skills and Attributes for Moving Up

Moving into senior leadership positions requires a combination of technical, strategic and people skills. Strategic Vision: From feature management to product portfolio management; from day-to-day to long-term planning; from prioritisation to goal setting; establishing a vision and linking it to execution. Leadership and People Management: From craftsmanship to scalable leadership skills, including mentoring, team building and conflict resolution.Financial Acumen: From feature profit and loss (P&L) to product P&L; from feature budgets to product budgeting; from feature revenue to product revenue; from feature-driven to sales-driven; from feature-based to product-based decisions. Influence and Negotiation: From feature feature negotiation to product-product negotiation; from feature feature influencing to product product influencing; from feature feature lobbying to product-product lobbying; developing the ability to influence senior executives and board members.Adaptability and Continuous Learning: From feature feature knowledge to product knowledge; from feature feature industry and market; from feature feature technology to the broader technology landscape; from feature feature lifecycle to product lifecycle; from feature feature to holistic product; from feature feature to customer feature feature; from feature feature to customer needs; from feature feature to products that users really like.

Building a Leadership Mindset

Consequently, the kind of mindset you need to transition into more senior leadership roles is quite different. Whereas a tactical mindset is geared towards execution, with an eye on the day-to-day, a strategic mindset is more attuned to long-term planning. In a nutshell, a strategic mindset allows executives to think beyond the immediate and address future trends, market shifts, and pitfalls, among other things. Essentially, it will help you lead your organisation according to its vision and set you up for sustainable growth.

Equally, they need to balance different styles of leadership. Sometimes, a boss has to be directive. They need to be clear about what they want, and set clear boundaries and expectations. Other times, the best leaders take a hands-off approach, and allow their team members to take ownership of problems and make autonomous decisions. This allows you to develop a culture that's conducive to autonomy and accountability, which is vital for innovation and creativity. The best leaders are flexible and can adapt to what their team needs to succeed in the context of the challenge they're facing.

A second cornerstone is the capacity to build', of collaboration, of trust. Good leaders seek ways to break down silos within organisations, to foster open communication and transparency between departments, to encourage team members to share their ideas, to speak out if they see something that could hurt the team, company or organisation, and work together to achieve the company's objectives. Without such collaboration, innovation becomes stifled.

18.5 How to Prepare for Leadership Roles

Leading a group of people takes preparation. Whether you are trying to move up the ladder or have just been promoted, there is some proactive personal development that you should engage in. First, set clear career goals. What do you want to be doing in five to 10 years? Develop a plan to get there, by not only strengthening your existing skill-set but also learning new ones. For example, a skill that might be critical at the director level but of little use at the line-level is strategic planning. Or, a skill that might be helpful in the line-level but that you might have little use for at the director level could be planning and organising. Finally, what are your team members, peers and direct reports saying about you? It is important to try to find out what others think your strengths and growth areas are. When talking to a coach or mentor, it might be a good idea to ask what others' perceptions are of your work style and behaviours, so that you can be prepared to update your personal development plan. If you follow these guidelines, you will be well-prepared for most leadership roles.

It's hard to overestimate the importance of a mentor and a network for personal development. A mentor who has trodden the path before you and can help you tackle tough choices can be invaluable, as can the network you build up around you, both inside and outside your organisation. The higher you want to climb, the more you need to rely on people who already occupy the heights. Go to conferences in your field, attend workshops, and participate in online forums and communities of practice to build your network and give yourself more visibility.

Developing a personal brand is also important for aspiring leaders. Publish articles, speak at conferences, or post insights on social media. Having a personal brand gives you more visibility, credibility and perceived power within your industry, which makes it easier to obtain mandates for leadership roles at a higher level.

Making the Move to Senior Leadership

Understanding the difference between internal promotions and external job opportunities is essential here. Internal promotions can be less stressful as you're familiar with the culture and teams. However, promotions often happen when someone who's already on the team is promoted. This requires you to shore up leadership brands long before a slot becomes available – and that means stretch assignments, volunteering for cross-departmental projects, proving you can be successful leading and managing a team, and so on.

By contrast, external opportunities can present the opportunity for quicker advancement and the chance to bring new ideas to new teams. If you're contemplating an external move, make sure your CV and LinkedIn profile are in top shape – be sure to highlight your accomplishments and leadership experience. Allow your interviews to focus on how you led projects, managed teams and delivered results. Be prepared to discuss your strategic orientation – and how you can bring value to a new organisation.

 Creating a portfolio of achievements can make you a more attractive candidate for advancement into leadership positions. Identify your accomplishments and collect metrics that serve as evidence of your success, particularly if you have launched a project, taken charge of an initiative, turned around a troubled project, resolved a conflict, or managed a crisis. These stories can provide concrete examples of what you have done as a leader when interviewing for a promotion.

Challenges of Leadership Roles

 The challenges of senior-level leadership are different. As a senior leader, you have more staff to manage, more stakeholders to report to and more things to be accountable for – including your failures. As a leader, you will be responsible for far more than individual projects – you will be responsible for the collective output of your teams. You will also be responsible for ensuring that your teams and their work are aligned with the vision and strategy of your organisation. This requires being able to delegate effectively, communicating clearly, and also inspiring and motivating. Managing larger teams often means having more personalities and skills to manage – which can also mean more conflict and misunderstandings. Being able to manage these conflicts, and navigate them diplomatically, is another critical leadership skill to master.

 A more significant aspect of leading at this level is greater accountability. As leaders are responsible not just for the success of a pet project, but for the performance of their department overall (eg, budgets, revenue, policies and regulations, and so on). The stakes are therefore higher and, consequently, leaders at this level need to have the courage of their convictions, make hard

127

calls and be prepared to make them under pressure. Knowing when to shift gears, cut losses or take a calculated risk are among their core competencies.

The handing of failure is a necessary part of leadership. No matter how good a plan might be, or what the data and projections show, things will go wrong. The best leaders learn from failure, and see it as an opportunity for learning and development. Leaders must encourage a culture that accepts failure as a part of learning, rather than a stumbling block.

The Role of a CPO in Shaping Company Strategy

The CPO is also pivotal to the process of setting the company's product strategy – that is, making sure that every product initiative takes into account the company's overall business strategy. Because the CPO is the most senior product person in the company, she has a responsibility to set the long-term vision for the product portfolio, articulating that vision to the rest of the company and helping the teams deliver on it. This entails close coordination with the other C-level executives, such as the CEO, CTO and CFO, to ensure the product strategy is aligned with the company's financial, technical and operational strategies.

One of the most central roles of a CPO is to define the product vision. What are the core problems the company is trying to solve for its customers? What's the roadmap to get there – what will the products do to solve these problems – and why? The CPO must articulate this vision and then communicate it to the various internal and external stakeholders to build agreement and alignment on the company's strategy.

He must also work closely with other executives, as product development doesn't happen in a vacuum. He must work with his marketing and sales colleagues in order to make sure that the features he's developing respond to the market's needs, can be sold to prospects, and are worth the cost. He must work with his engineering colleagues in order to make sure that the features can be developed within the technology they're working with, and are feasible to produce. And he must work with his finance colleagues in order to understand the implications of product decisions on his company's pricing strategy, revenue projections, and cost base. The good CPO is someone who can balance the need for innovation with the need to push the company's money as far as it can go. When done well, it can help fuel growth.

The second role for the CPO is to be the champion of innovation. This is about creating an organisational culture that encourages experimentation, creativity and continuous improvement. By keeping up with market trends, new technologies and consumer behaviours, the CPO can help the company keep ahead of shifts in the market.

18.9 Practical Steps to Climbing the Ladder

If you want to move up the ladder to leadership in product management, it helps to make strategic career moves, develop skills and grow as a person. One of the most powerful ways to do this, and demonstrate to others that you have what it takes, is through stretch assignments. Stretch assignments are those that develop your humanity by extrapolating on what you already know how to do and expanding your skillset and scope of responsibility to something that you don't yet know how to do. Think of a stretch assignment as a type of road that doesn't yet exist but would be useful to have. It could be a two-lane highway or a large multi-lane freeway.

Getting feedback is another important aspect of personal and professional development. By asking for regular feedback from your peers, your mentor, and your supervisors, you'll find out where you need to improve and how people are perceiving your strengths. Whatever feedback you get, it's important that you work on it and show that you're willing to change, since this is an important skill and quality to display for someone who wants to lead.

Certifications, courses and education might also be helpful in advancing your career. Taking a leadership class or an MBA, or learning a new skill through a professional certification (eg, in project management, agile methodologies, data analysis) might help you stand out when applying for senior positions. They might also demonstrate that you continue to develop your own abilities and expertise.

Don't forget about networking. Establishing positive relationships with your colleagues, fellow professionals and mentors can lead to new opportunities, pave the way through difficult times, and help you decide how to move forward. Go to industry events, join professional organisations, and blog online to meet others and remain connected with them.

Chapter 19: 20 Case Studies & Practice Questions

Learning Through Real-World Examples
Product management interviews can be a bit intimidating because the types of questions are much deeper than you'll encounter in engineering interviews. This is because, at its core, product management involves making decisions across a wide range of topics, like answering strategic questions, making data-driven decisions, and scaling products for the highest impact. Gaining insight into how real PMs tackle these challenges will be extremely useful to have in your pocket when you go into your own product management interview, and that's why we're excited to spend this chapter delving into practical case studies. I'll walk you through several interview questions that I've heard from top companies such as Google, Meta , Netflix, and others, and explain how candidates answered them successfully.

18.2 Product Strategy and Market Adaptation

Case Study 1: Navigating Product Pivots in a Competitive Market

Key Interview Question (Actual Google Question): "Your company is building an e-commerce platform and you are managing a project related to this product. Halfway through the project, a new competitor enters the market and starts to offer a similar service, but with a distinctive feature. How would you pivot your product strategy?"

Example Response: "While working on a shopping app, I was once tasked with monitoring a new app that provided curated shopping recommendations. We did research with the aim of identifying the competitor's unique selling points (USPs) and compared them against user feedback on our app. Rather than replicate the competitor's feature, we could focus on the checkout experience, given that our user data showed that this was a major pain point. We redesigned our checkout process and added a new 'buy-now-pay-later' feature. These changes translated into a 15 per cent increase in conversions within a quarter."

Case Study 2: Handling Product Failure and Learning From It

Key Interview Question: "What about a time when a product you managed wasn't successful? What did you learn?"

Example Response: "I was the leader of a team building a social networking feature that was designed to increase engagement on our platform. After launch, it had low adoption and users indicated they were confused about the value. We collected feedback through surveys and identified two main issues: onboarding wasn't great and it wasn't integrated into core product experiences. I led the team to sunset the feature and instead focus on the core user journey, which resulted in a 20 per cent increase in user engagement. This experience taught me the importance of validating ideas early and often through extensive user testing."

18.3 Data-Driven Decision Making and Feature Prioritization

Case Study 3: Building a Data-Driven Product Roadmap

Key Interview Question (Actual Meta Question): "How do you use data to drive your product roadmap? How do you decide what features to work on?"

Example Response: "The RICE Framework is a good tool to get started with. At a previous job, we did NPS surveys and used analytics tools to gather user feedback on features. We found that people struggled to get past the onboarding phase of the product. This was costing us a lot of retention. I used RICE (Reach, Impact, Confidence, Effort) to prioritise a new onboarding experience over other features people asked for. We A/B tested it and found 30% more people completed the onboarding. After that, I always understood the importance of data-driven prioritisation of user retention."

Case Study 4: Driving Growth with Metrics and Experimentation

Key Interview Question (Actual Netflix Question): "How would you measure the success of a new feature and then iterate on it?"

Example Response: "When we introduced a content recommendation feature at Netflix, we measured the effect on engagement by comparing user interaction metrics (such as watch time). We used a light-touch approach to optimise the algorithm. For example, when we began to see lower engagement among new users, we tailored the recommendations more aggressively for that user segment, driving up watch time by 25 per cent. DAU/MAU (along with metrics like churn rate) were key metrics used to determine success of the feature."

18.4 User-Centric Development and Retention

Case Study 5: Mastering User Retention and Engagement

Key Interview Question (Actual Meta Question): "How do you ensure user retention and improve product stickiness?"

Example Response: "At Meta, we came up with features such as Facebook Stories that helped keep users engaged. To retain users, features that increased engagement without annoying the user with notifications were prioritised. Adding controls for how often users wanted to be notified helped keep them engaged. We found that features that helped users control their experience lowered churn rates, especially among the younger age groups."

Case Study 6: Incorporating Customer Feedback into Product Development

Key Interview Question: "How do you use and react to client feedback to better shape product development?"

Example Response: "Qualitative methods include asking questions, for instance via surveys and users interviews, and quantitative methods include looking at product data, for instance to find out how users interact with the product. In the SaaS company I worked for, we heard a similar request from our customers over and over again: can we get more flexible billing options? I led the team to build such an adaptive billing system for different business scenarios, and we observed a 10 per cent increase in customer retention three months after the launch."

18.5 Leading Cross-Functional Teams and Collaboration

Case Study 7: Leading Cross-Functional Collaboration

Key Interview Question: "Tell me about a time when you had to work across different teams to deliver a product, and how you ensured successful alignment?"

Example Response: "When revamping the mobile app for our product, with overlapping responsibilities with engineering, design, marketing and customer support, I did a roadmap exercise, where I created a shared roadmap, along with weekly stand-ups to keep everybody on the same page. At an important juncture, the design team was unable to iterate on a section of the product because of a technical constraint from the engineering team. So I facilitated a design sprint: I got both the teams in a room to brainstorm solutions to the problem. Eventually, the redesign was done on time, and post-launch data showed a 40 per cent increase in user engagement."

Case Study 8: Navigating Remote Teams and Global Collaboration

Key Interview Question: "How do you handle cross-functional teams remotely or globally?"

Example Response: "When leading a distributed team and launching an app across the globe, communication is key, and setting expectations early helps your team perform at their best. I leveraged global collaborative tools such as Slack and Jira to empower my team to work together, and held a virtual stand-up in three different time zones to ensure global alignment and reduce friction. This allowed us to launch in three regions, simultaneously."

18.6 AI and Emerging Technologies in Product Management

Case Study 9: Incorporating AI into Product Strategy

Key Interview Question (Actual Google Question): "How would you incorporate AI into one of Google's consumer products (eg, Google Search, Google Assistant)?"

Example Response: "For Google Search, I would use AI to enhance personalising query by utilising natural language processing (NLP) to better interpret the user search intent. For example, if the user was to search for 'best running shoes', AI could personalise the search results based on their previous search history or location to provide higher user satisfaction and engagement."

Case Study 10: Leveraging AI for Product Insights and Personalization

Key Interview Question (Actual Netflix Question): "How would you improve the recommendations on Netflix to better engage a screen-addicted teenage boy?"

Example Response: "Aside from adapting to viewing history, AI algorithms could personalise content recommendations to the user's mood and context. For example, what if a service paired passive viewing (just watching) with active viewing (engaging with content via interactions like clicking, searching and skipping) to gather real-time feedback on user preferences? This would enable recommendations to be much more dynamic ('if you liked this, then you'll love this, but if you're in this mood and context, you might prefer this'). At the same time, ongoing collection of these data points would also allow for a more refined experience where the service becomes an on-demand platform for more accurately matching users with their preferred content and experiences."

18.7 Culture and Team Dynamics

Case Study 11: Aligning Product Strategy with Company Culture

Key Interview Question (Actual Google Question): "How do you ensure that your product strategy is aligned with the company's culture and values?"

Example Response: "If you are working on a sustainability initiative at Google, such as mine, it is important to make sure that your product features are consistent with the company's self-image as a powerhouse of environmental responsibility. For example, designing Google Home devices to be extremely energy-efficient reinforces the green 'culture' of the company. Using a technical feature to reinforce cultural values supports the business positioning of the product while also increasing in-house support."

18.8 Product Scaling and International Expansion

Case Study 12: Scaling a Product for International Markets

Key Interview Question: "How do you approach expanding a successful product into international regions?"

Example Response: "After scaling a health and wellness app into three European markets, ensuring the ability to speak the user's language and adhering to their content preferences was key to resonating with new audiences. Our marketing campaigns were tailored to local trends, while also remaining GDPRaudiences. Our marketing campaigns were tailored to local trends, while also remaining GDPR compliant. In six months, we were able to reach 30 per cent higher regional downloads and expand into three new markets."

18.9 Handling Scope Creep in Product Development

Case Study 13: Managing Scope Creep in a Project

Key Interview Question: "How do you handle scope creep in a project?"

Example Response: "To mitigate the risk of scope creep, if it occurs, I would first communicate any impacts to the timelines and resource requirements to stakeholders, then assess the new requests against the objectives of the product, and determine if they can be deferred to later releases. By establishing the priorities up front, I help to avoid scope creep."

18.10 Managing Negative User Feedback

Case Study 14: Handling Negative User Feedback

Key Interview Question: "Describe a situation where you received negative feedback from a user. How did you respond to the feedback?"

Example Response: "One of my previous projects had some UX problems, we received feedback that users found a feature too complex to use. We organized a user testing plan to collect qualitative feedback and evaluated that the onboarding process had too many steps. We modified the user flow to have fewer steps, and in the next product iteration, satisfaction scores increased by 20%."

18.11 Improving User Retention Through Experimentation

Case Study 15: Experimenting to Improve Retention Rates

Key Interview Question: "You've launched a new feature, and it's not as engaging as you expected. What are you going to do to increase engagement?"

Example Response: "I'd start by looking at the data to understand who the non-engagers are and why they're non-engagers, then possibly follow up with some user interviews or a survey to get some qualitative feedback. After doing that, I'd probably try out iterating on things like the UI or the messaging around the feature to try to drive engagement up."

18.12 Prioritizing Features for Competing User Demands

Case Study 16: Balancing Feature Requests and Resources

Key Interview Question: "You have two high-priority feature requests: one from the sales team for a new feature that can help to close one of the biggest deals of this quarter, and one from existing users for a performance improvement that reduces churn. Which one would you prioritize, and why?"

Example Response: "I would assess the business outcome potential of the requests. The sales-driven request would lead to a short-term revenue bump, but the performance improvement would lead to long-term user retention. With a RICE framework, I would prioritize the feature that has the highest potential for impact and the longest retention."

18.13 Leading Through Change in a Product Pivot

Case Study 17: Navigating a Major Product Pivot

Key Interview Question: "Describe a time when your team had to make a product pivot. How did you deal with the change?"

Example Response: "I led a team in one project where market conditions were shifting rapidly, and we had to pivot our strategy. I took the team through a re-prioritization exercise and realigned the product to the new market requirements. We re-scoped the product to focus on our most viable features and communicated the reasons for pivoting and involved the team in key decisions, so they felt part of the process and recognized that they had the ability to adapt and succeed."

18.14 Using Data to Inform Product Decisions

Case Study 18: Data-Driven Product Decisions

Key Interview Question: "How do you use data to inform product decisions?"

Example Response: "I use both qualitative and quantitative data. I rely on metrics like user retention, churn rates, and engagement to prioritize product features, while qualitative feedback from user interviews indicates pain points. We are always running A/B tests on product changes to confirm assumptions and make data-driven decisions."

18.15 Designing Products for Accessibility

Case Study 19: Incorporating Accessibility into Product Design

Key Interview Question: "What features would you want in a product to make it more usable by people with disabilities?"

Example Response: "My first step would be to do some user research with disabled users so that I can understand their particular pain points. I would also make sure that the product adheres to accessibility guidelines such as WCAG 2.1 and has features like keyboard navigation, screen reader support, and the ability to adjust colors. I would also do regular user testing with real users to make sure that these features provide the desired benefits."

18.16 Prioritizing in Resource-Constrained Environments

Case Study 20: Managing Limited Resources

Key Interview Question: "You're running a product with limited engineering resources, and you have to choose between investing time into developing new features or improving on existing performance. What would you do?"

Example Response: "I would try to assess the impact on important metrics like user satisfaction, as well as business metrics such as churn, revenue or engagement. If improved performance solves user pains that are critical to the business, then it might be more important. But if a new feature unlocks new revenue or engagement, that might take precedence as well. I would try to use the data to steer the decision."

18.17 Using KPIs to Track Product Success

Case Study 21: Setting KPIs for Success

Key Interview Question: "What KPIs would you track to measure the success of a new product?"

Example Response: "I would track user adoption rates, retention, and engagement: DAU, percentage of users who performed a particular action, NPS from users, and revenue growth over time; I would also track feature-specific metrics like click-through rate."

18.18 Designing Onboarding for Complex SaaS Products

Case Study 22: Simplifying SaaS Onboarding

Key Interview Question: "How would you design an onboarding experience for a complicated SaaS application?"

Example Response: "For a complex SaaS product, I would create a modular onboarding experience, which starts with a high-level walkthrough of the core features of the product and has more detailed tutorials on specific advanced features triggered by user actions. Engagement through tooltips and help centers can be done continuously to ensure that users don't feel overwhelmed and can learn one piecè at a time."

18.19 Defining Product Strategy in a Competitive Market

Case Study 23: Developing Product Strategy Under Competition

Key Interview Question: "How do you create a product strategy when a competitor enters your market with a similar product?"

Example Response: "I'd want us to try to differentiate our product with features that fill unmet user needs or simply enhance the user experience. I'd do a competitive analysis and user research to define what uniquely valuable thing we're offering, then use the same data to help us prioritize new features that give us an edge while we continue to iterate on core functionality."

18.20 Managing Feature Requests from Stakeholders

Case Study 24: Balancing Stakeholder Expectations

Key Interview Question: "How do you prioritize feature requests from different stakeholders with conflicting priorities?"

Example Response: "I would ask for input from each of the stakeholders, and try to assess what the impact of that request will be on the business as well as the user experience. I would then prioritize based on the degree of alignment with the product's goal, and to what extent the end users are benefiting. Clear communication is important as well – try to convey to stakeholders why you are prioritizing some things over others."

Closing Statements

With this journey nearing the end, I hope you enjoyed this book as much as I did writing it, and feel like you learned something and now feel more confident to sit through the next product manager interview. In this last chapter, we looked at what makes a good product manager, starting off with product strategy and market challenges, leading and innovating, and finally, we examined how data decisions need to be incorporated.

The reality is that product management continues to change: with new technologies such as AI, user expectations, and needs in international markets. What does not change is the need for thoughtful, empathetic, courageous, data-driven leadership. We've put the research in this book to properly outline the right context from you to inspire yourself from when tackling interviews. The goal is not to give you all the answers - but to make you think and to keep in mind this additional perspective.

But don't forget, a product management interview is just the start of your journey. Successful product managers must learn to constantly grow, overcome the challenges of unscripted leadership, inspire cross-functional teams, and build products that make a real difference in the lives of our users. Once you've gotten the job, the interview is over – the real work of figuring out how to become a market guardian, changing with the market, comes next.

I invite you to keep sharpening your tools, follow your curiosity, and join me in the messiness of product management, where every product manager is just making it up as they go along: the tools you've built in this guide are just the beginning of your journey towards your own space in our weird, wonderful and exciting field.

And good luck to you – not just for the interview, but for your career as a product manager as you go on to deliver all those features and innovations that will make you and your company successful.

Made in the USA
Monee, IL
26 November 2024

71299176R00085